Caligrafía
para niños en inglés

"**Caligrafía para niños en inglés**" es un libro que aprovecha la capacidad de aprendizaje rápido de los niños en desarrollo que aprenden inglés como segunda lengua. Ofrece actividades estimulantes en números, caligrafía y lectura en inglés, estableciendo una base sólida para su crecimiento intelectual y emocional mientras exploran el mundo de las palabras en un contexto bilingüe.

Si has disfrutado este libro con tus pequeñitos, tu opinión es fundamental! Te invitamos a calificarnos y dejar un mensaje, así seguiremos mejorando y ofreciendo publicaciones cada día más enriquecedoras.
¡Gracias por compartir la magia de aprender juntos!

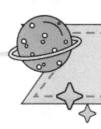

HELP OUR FRIEND THE SNAIL REACH ITS FOOD

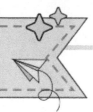

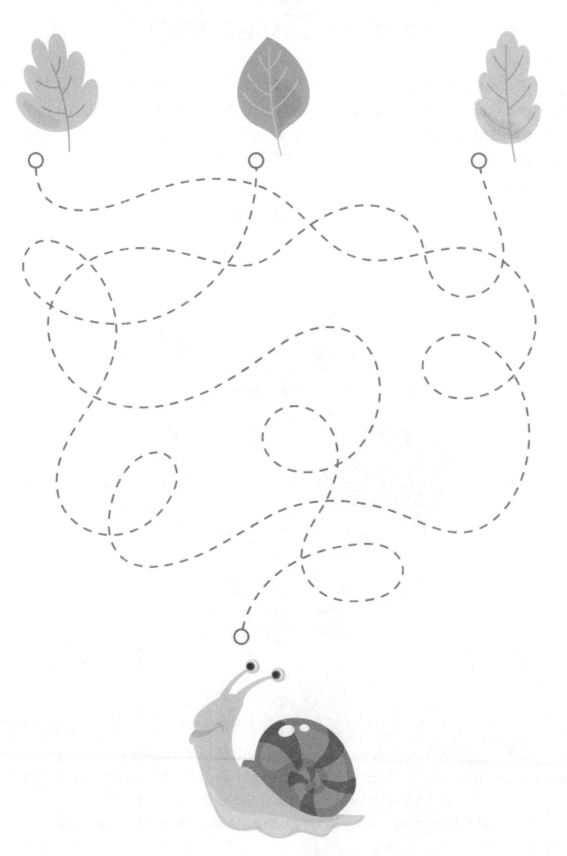

HELP THE FISHERMAN
CATCH THE FISH

TRACE THE STARS AND TRAJECTORY OF THE ROCKETS IN SPACE

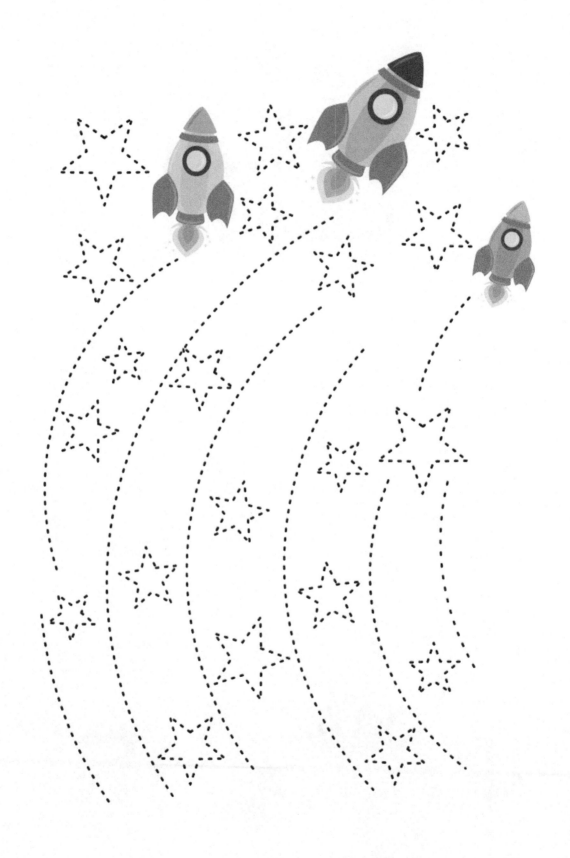

TRACE THE PATH OF EACH
OF THE VEHICLES

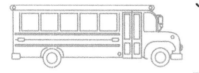

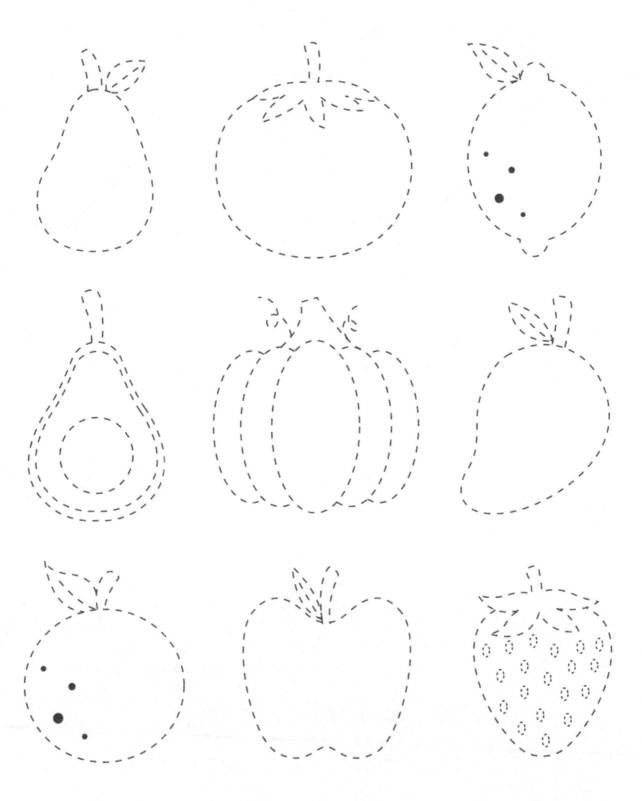

 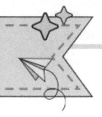

The **uppercase** vowels

A E I O U

The **uppercase** consonants

B C D F G

H J K L M

N P Q R S

T V W X Y

Z

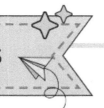
The **lowercase** vowels

a e i o u

The **lowercase** consonants

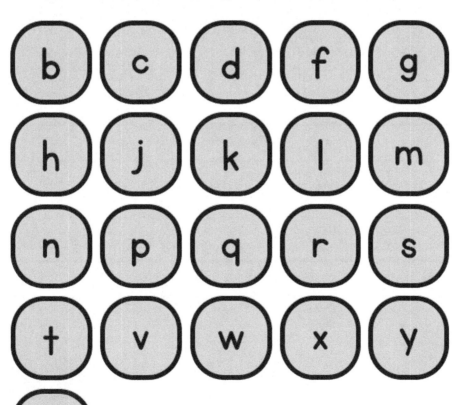

b c d f g

h j k l m

n p q r s

t v w x y

z

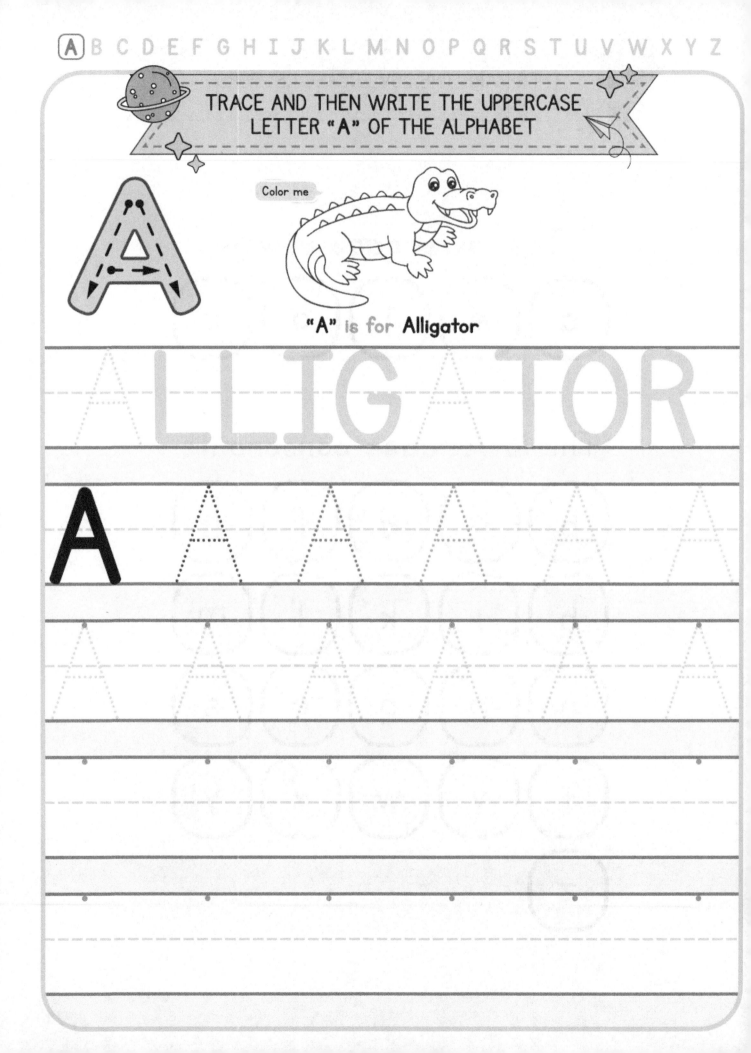

TRACE AND THEN WRITE THE UPPERCASE
LETTER "A" OF THE ALPHABET

Color me

"A" is for **Alligator**

TRACE AND THEN WRITE THE LOWERCASE LETTER "a" OF THE ALPHABET

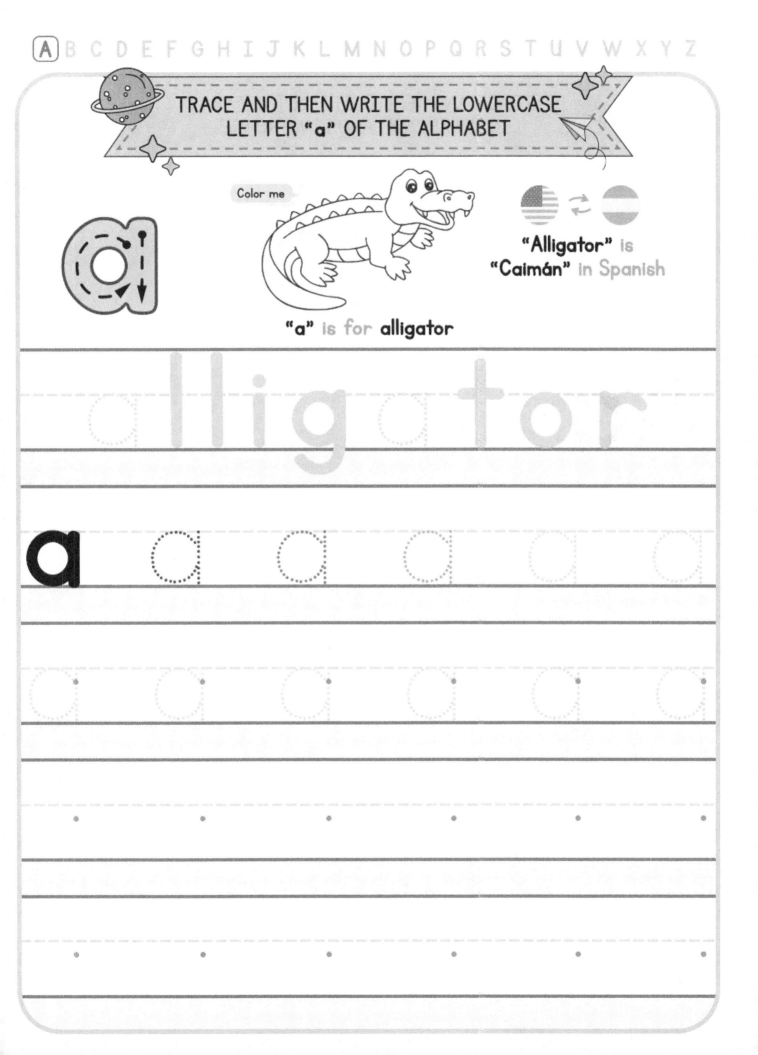

Color me

"a" is for **alligator**

"Alligator" is "Caimán" in Spanish

TRACE AND REPEAT THE LETTER "A"
IN UPPERCASE AND LOWERCASE

Aa

COMPLETE THIS SERIES OF ACTIVITIES TO REINFORCE WHAT YOU HAVE LEARNED

1 Circle all the letters "A,a"

C R a B
A d R e
w B a v
d C A
a e w V

2 Color these things that are written with the letter "A,a"

Airplane

Acorn

Anchor

Alien

3 Complete the word with the missing letter

nim l

nt

pple

4 Draw something that begins or contains the letter "A,a"

TRACE AND THEN WRITE THE UPPERCASE LETTER "B" OF THE ALPHABET

Color me

"B" is for Bee

B E E

B B B B B B

TRACE AND THEN WRITE THE LOWERCASE LETTER "b" OF THE ALPHABET

Color me

"b" is for **bee**

"Bee" is "Abeja" in Spanish

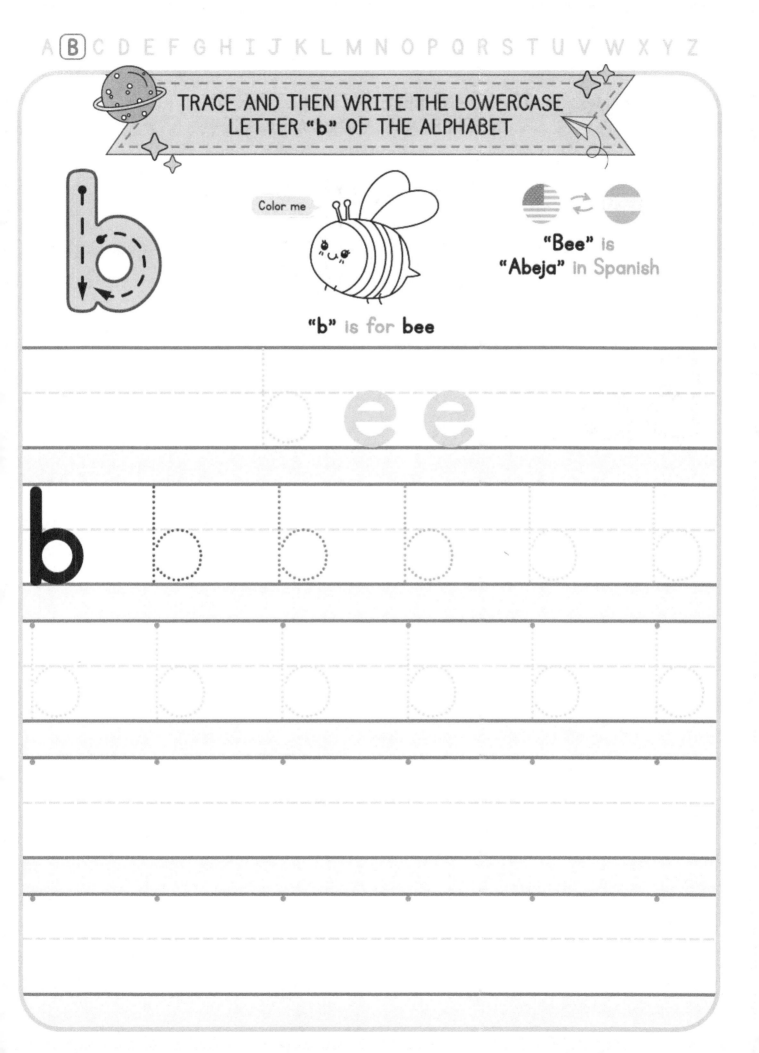

 C D E F G H I J K L M N O P Q R S T U V W X Y Z

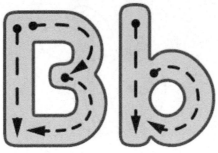

Bb

Bb Bb Bb Bb

COMPLETE THIS SERIES OF ACTIVITIES
TO REINFORCE WHAT YOU HAVE LEARNED

1 Circle all the letters "B,b"

2 Color these things that are written with the letter "B,b"

Bucket

Books

Bear

Boat

3 Complete the word with the missing letter

lue

ike

anana

4 Draw something that begins or contains the letter "B,b"

A B C D E F G H I J K L M N O P Q R S T U V W X Y Z

Color me

"C" is for Cat

CAT

C C C C C C C

TRACE AND THEN WRITE THE LOWERCASE LETTER "c" OF THE ALPHABET

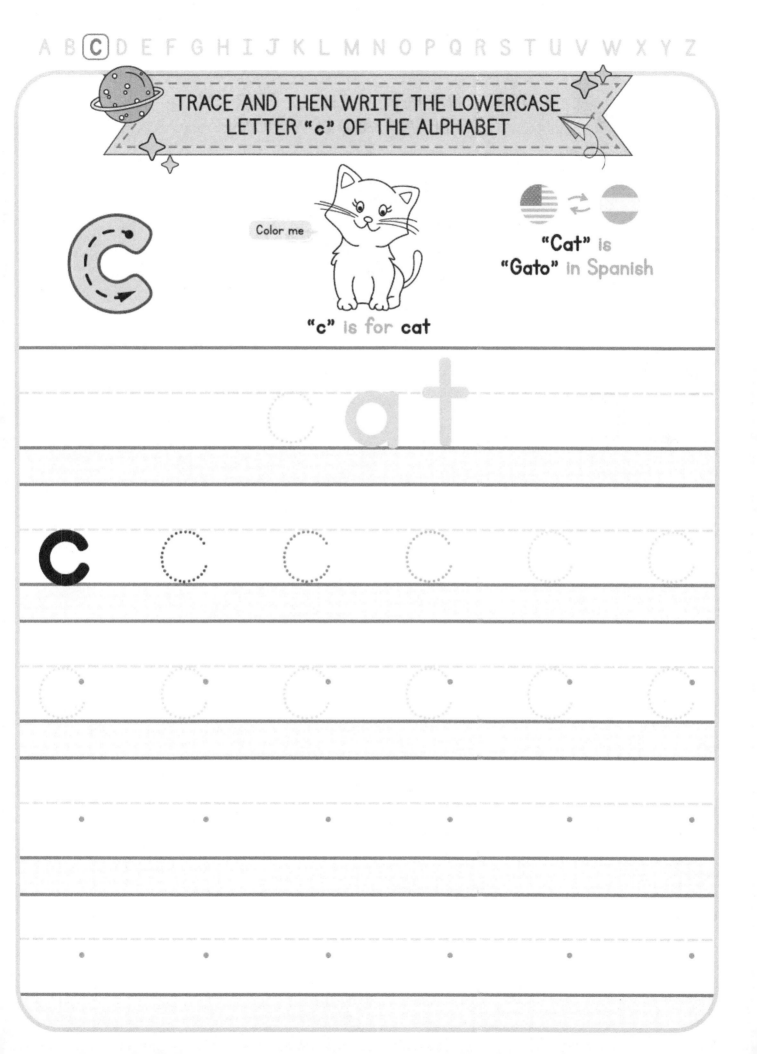

Color me

"c" is for **cat**

"Cat" is
"Gato" in Spanish

TRACE AND REPEAT THE LETTER "C" IN UPPERCASE AND LOWERCASE

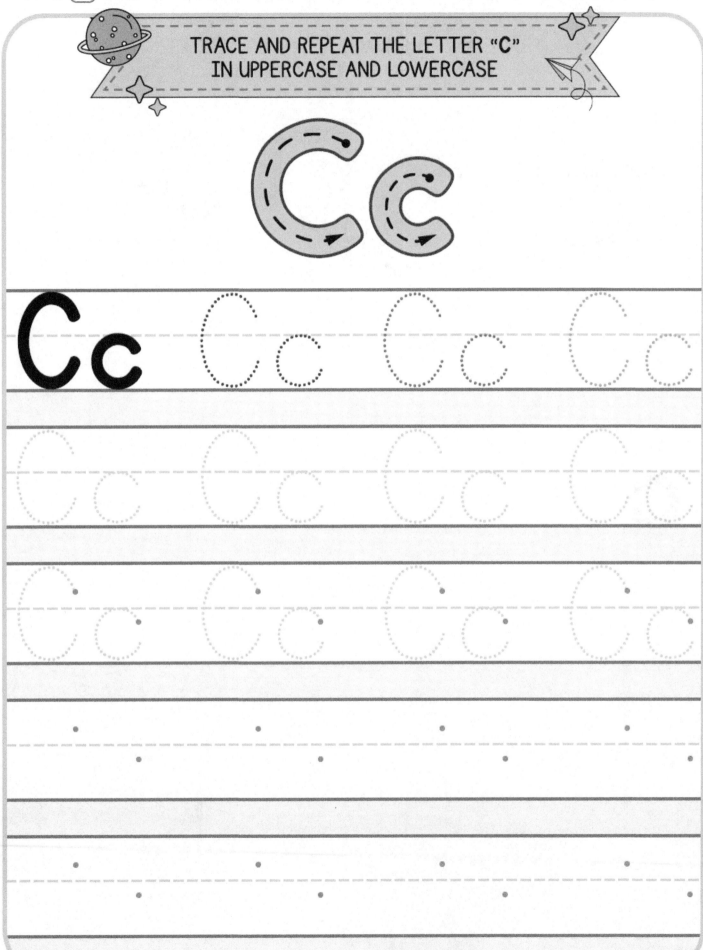

COMPLETE THIS SERIES OF ACTIVITIES
TO REINFORCE WHAT YOU HAVE LEARNED

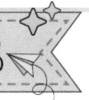

1 Circle all the letters "C,c"

2 Color these things that are written with the letter "C,c"

Crab

Cake

Car

Clown

3 Complete the word with the missing letter

oat

loud

lo k

4 Draw something that begins or contains the letter "C,c"

TRACE AND THEN WRITE THE UPPERCASE LETTER "D" OF THE ALPHABET

Color me

"D" is for Dog

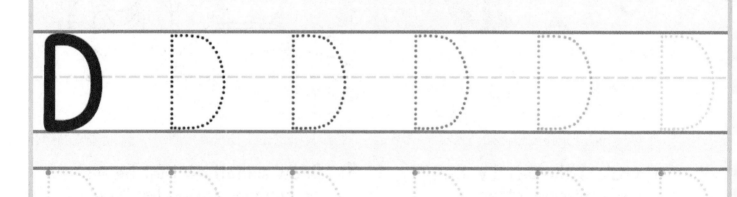

TRACE AND THEN WRITE THE LOWERCASE LETTER "d" OF THE ALPHABET

Color me

"d" is for **dog**

"Dog" is
"Perro" in Spanish

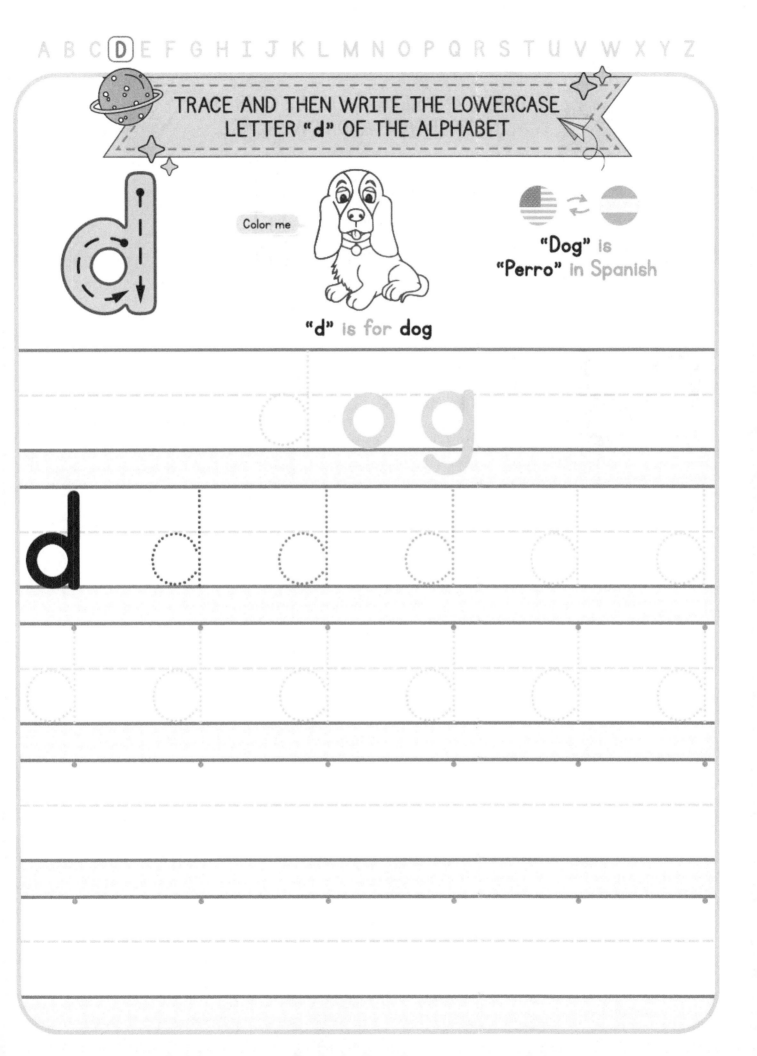

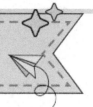

TRACE AND REPEAT THE LETTER "D" IN UPPERCASE AND LOWERCASE

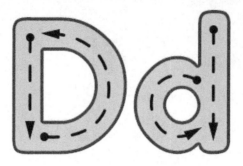

Dd Dd Dd Dd

COMPLETE THIS SERIES OF ACTIVITIES
TO REINFORCE WHAT YOU HAVE LEARNED

1 Circle all the letters "D,d"

2 Color these things that are written with the letter "D,d"

Duck

Doll

Dolphin

Door

Donut

3 Complete the word with the missing letter

iamond

ay

ance

4 Draw something that begins or contains the letter "D,d"

TRACE AND THEN WRITE THE UPPERCASE LETTER "E" OF THE ALPHABET

Color me

"E" is for Elephant

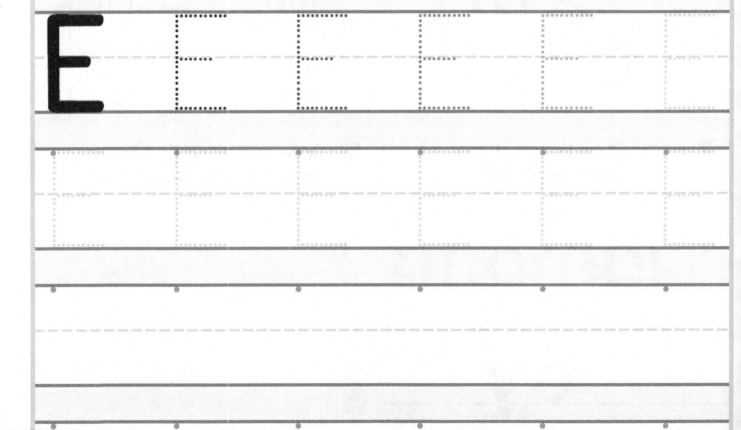

TRACE AND THEN WRITE THE LOWERCASE LETTER "e" OF THE ALPHABET

Color me

"e" is for **elephant**

"Elephant" is
"Elefante" in Spanish

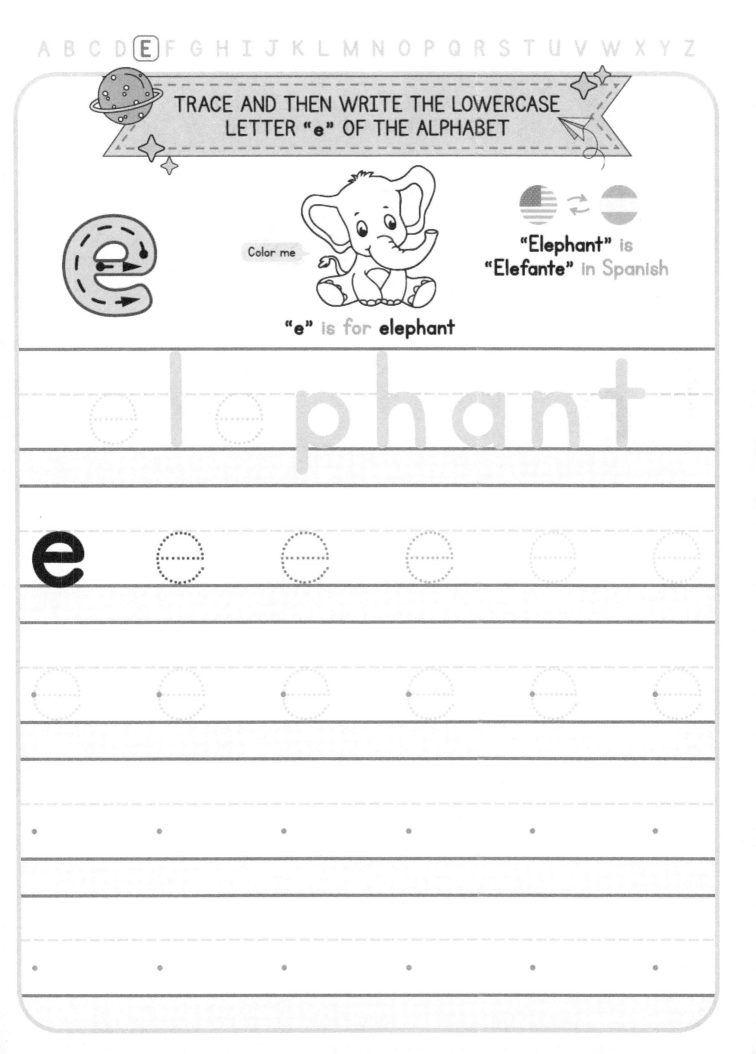

TRACE AND REPEAT THE LETTER "E"
IN UPPERCASE AND LOWERCASE

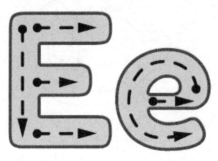

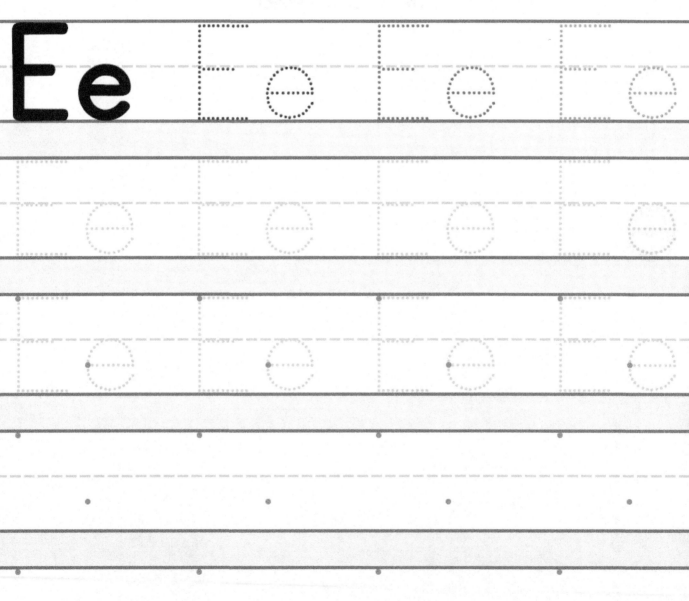

TRACE AND REPEAT THE LETTER "E"
IN UPPERCASE AND LOWERCASE

COMPLETE THIS SERIES OF ACTIVITIES TO REINFORCE WHAT YOU HAVE LEARNED

1   Circle all the letters "E,e"

2   Color these things that are written with the letter "E,e"

Envelope

Earth

Elf

Excavator

3   Complete the word with the missing letter

gg

asy

at

4   Draw something that begins or contains the letter "E,e"

TRACE AND THEN WRITE THE UPPERCASE LETTER "F" OF THE ALPHABET

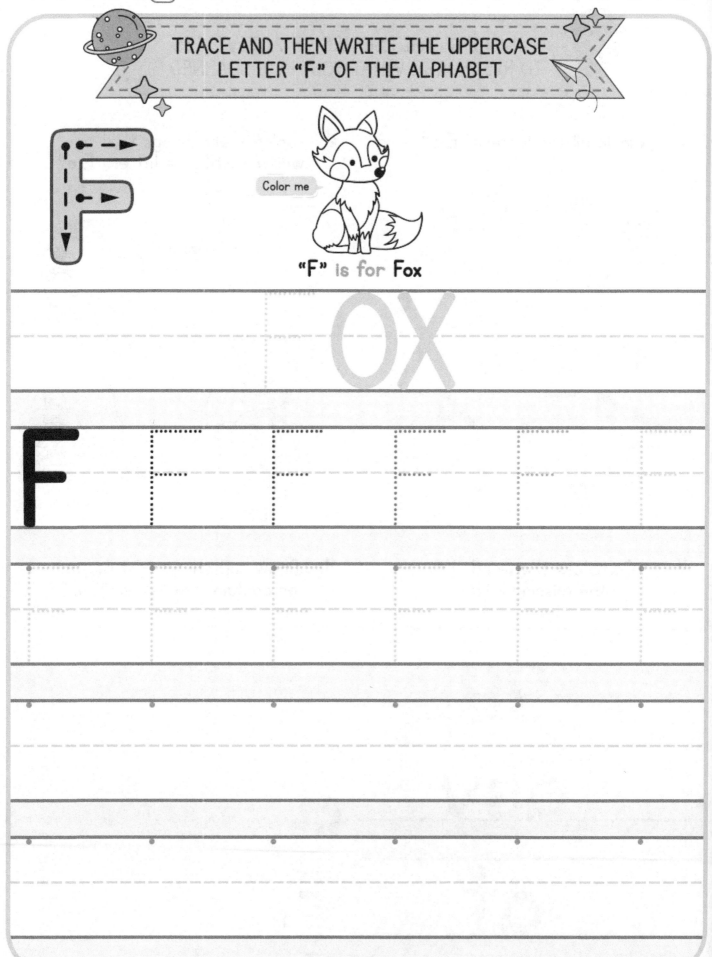

Color me

"F" is for Fox

TRACE AND THEN WRITE THE LOWERCASE LETTER "f" OF THE ALPHABET

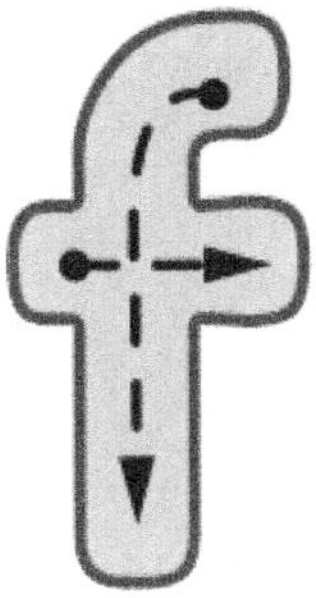

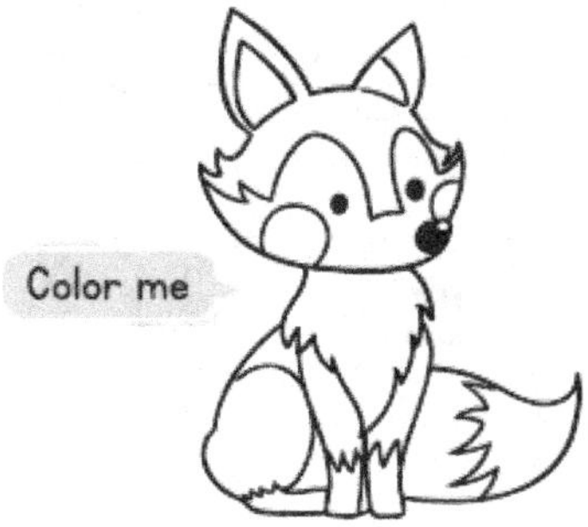

Color me

"f" is for fox

"Fox" is "Zorro" in Spanish

o x

f   f   f   f   f   f

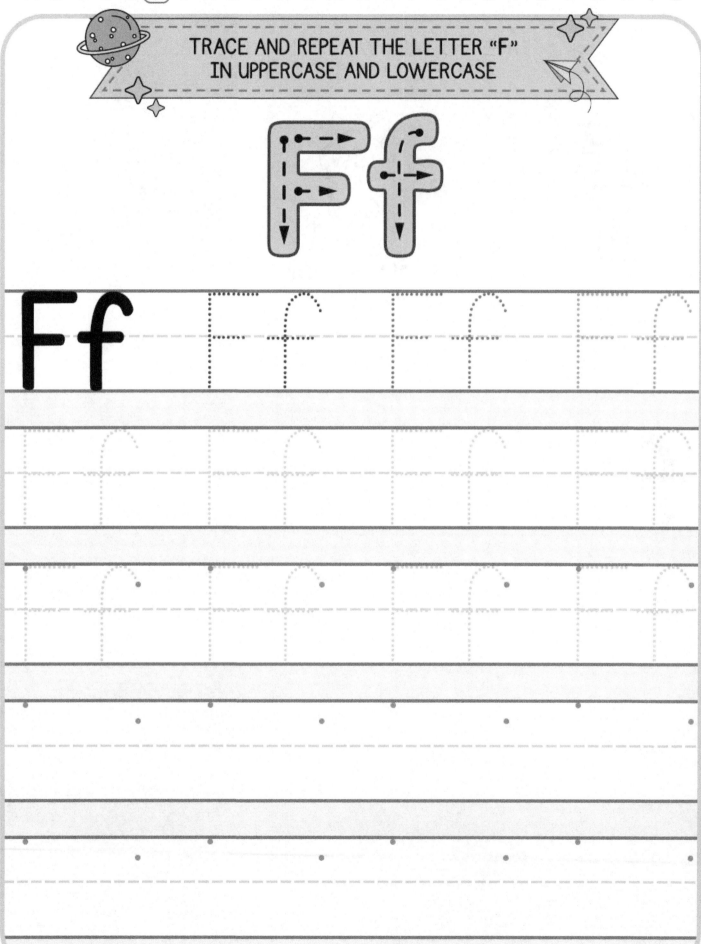

TRACE AND REPEAT THE LETTER "F"
IN UPPERCASE AND LOWERCASE

A B C D E F G H I J K L M N O P Q R S T U V W X Y Z

COMPLETE THIS SERIES OF ACTIVITIES TO REINFORCE WHAT YOU HAVE LEARNED

1 Circle all the letters "F,f"

2 Color these things that are written with the letter "F,f"

Frog

Fire truck

Feather

Flamingo

3 Complete the word with the missing letter

ruit

arm

riend

4 Draw something that begins or contains the letter "F,f"

TRACE AND THEN WRITE THE UPPERCASE LETTER "G" OF THE ALPHABET

Color me

"G" is for **Goat**

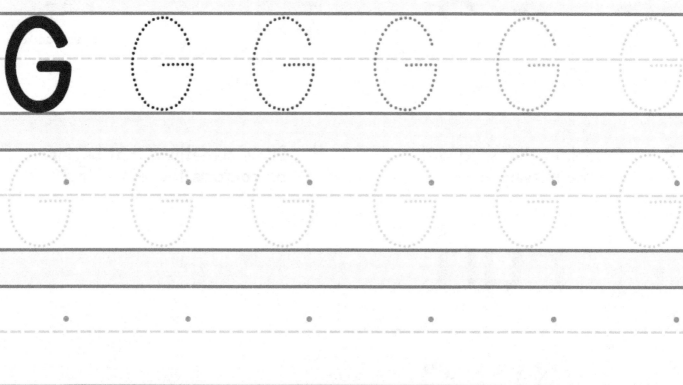

TRACE AND THEN WRITE THE LOWERCASE LETTER "g" OF THE ALPHABET

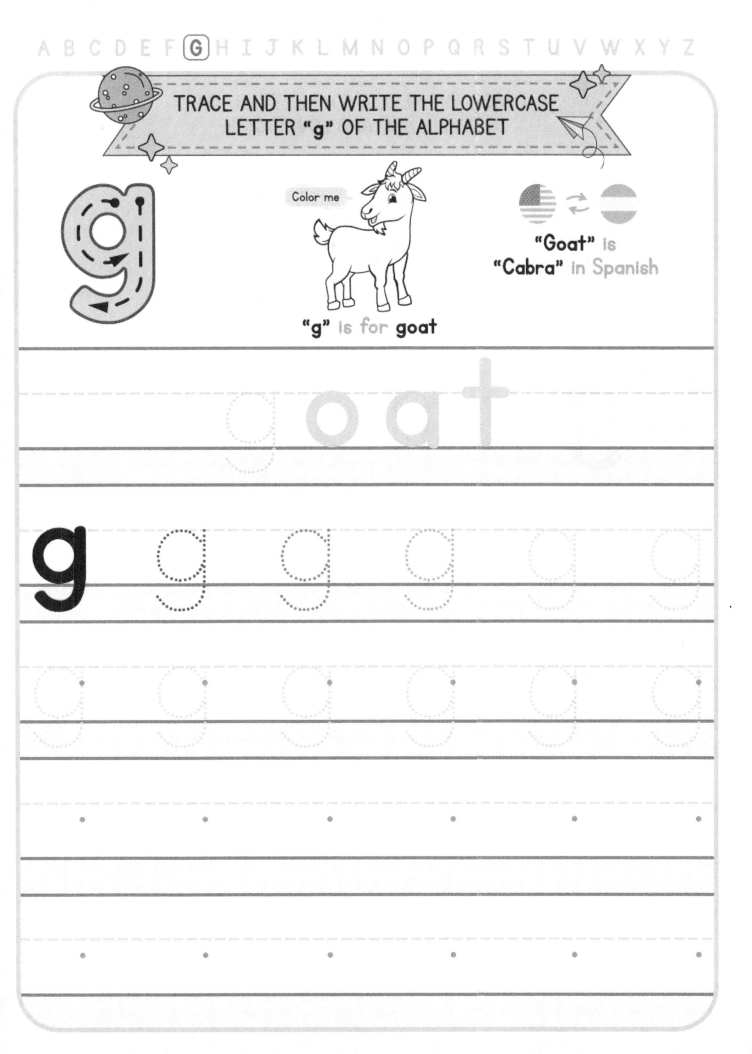

Color me

"g" is for **goat**

"Goat" is "Cabra" in Spanish

g oat

g g g g g g

TRACE AND REPEAT THE LETTER "G" IN UPPERCASE AND LOWERCASE

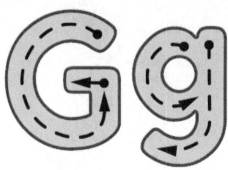

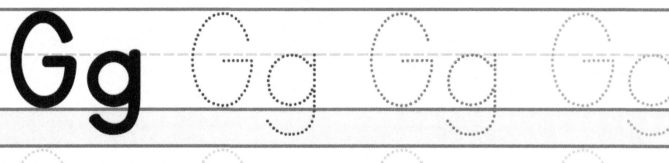

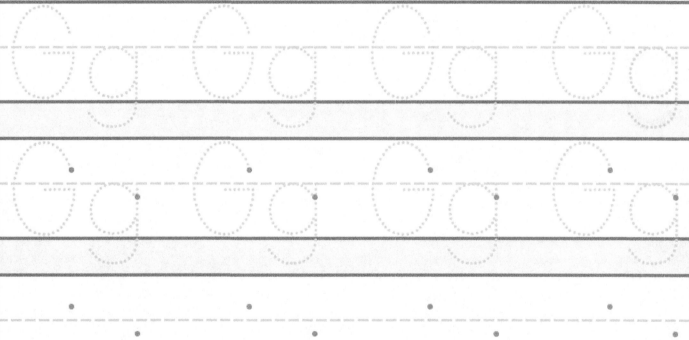

COMPLETE THIS SERIES OF ACTIVITIES
TO REINFORCE WHAT YOU HAVE LEARNED

1 Circle all the letters "G,g"

2 Color these things that are written with the letter "G,g"

Grapes

Grasshopper

Guitar

Gift

3 Complete the word with the missing letter

reen

arden

ame

4 Draw something that begins or contains the letter "G,g"

TRACE AND THEN WRITE THE UPPERCASE LETTER "H" OF THE ALPHABET

Color me

"H" is for **House**

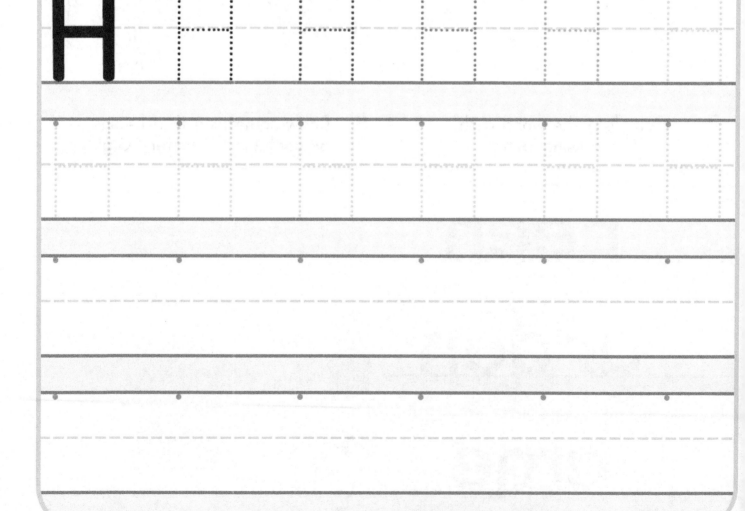

TRACE AND THEN WRITE THE LOWERCASE LETTER "h" OF THE ALPHABET

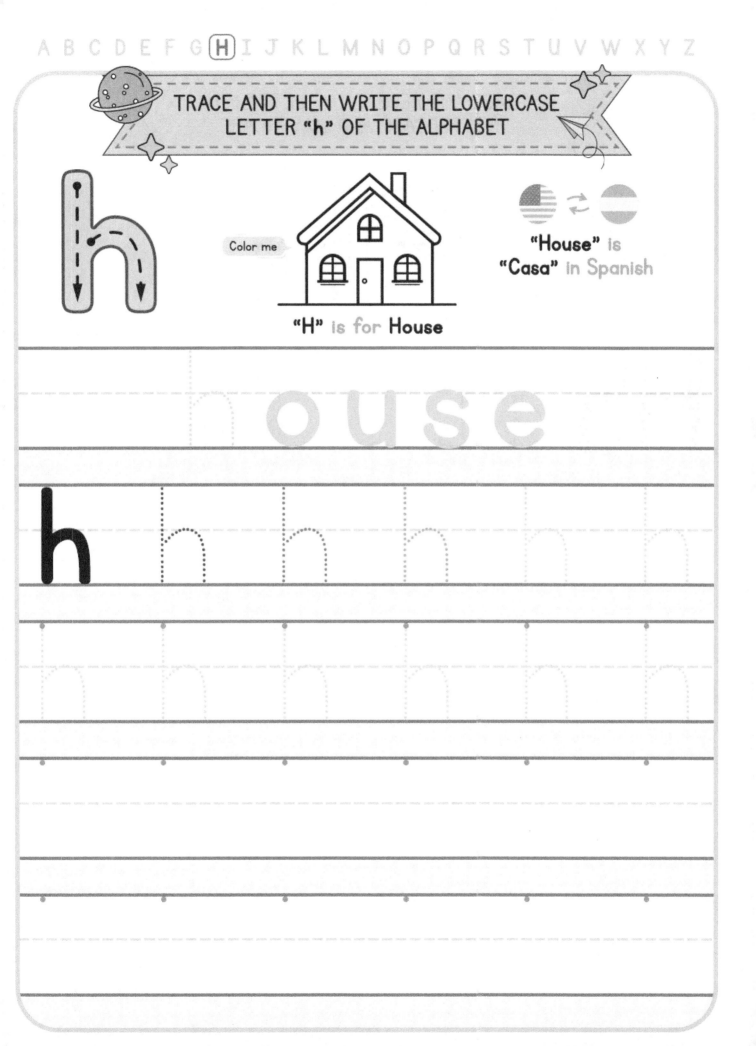

Color me

"H" is for **House**

"House" is
"Casa" in Spanish

h o u s e

h

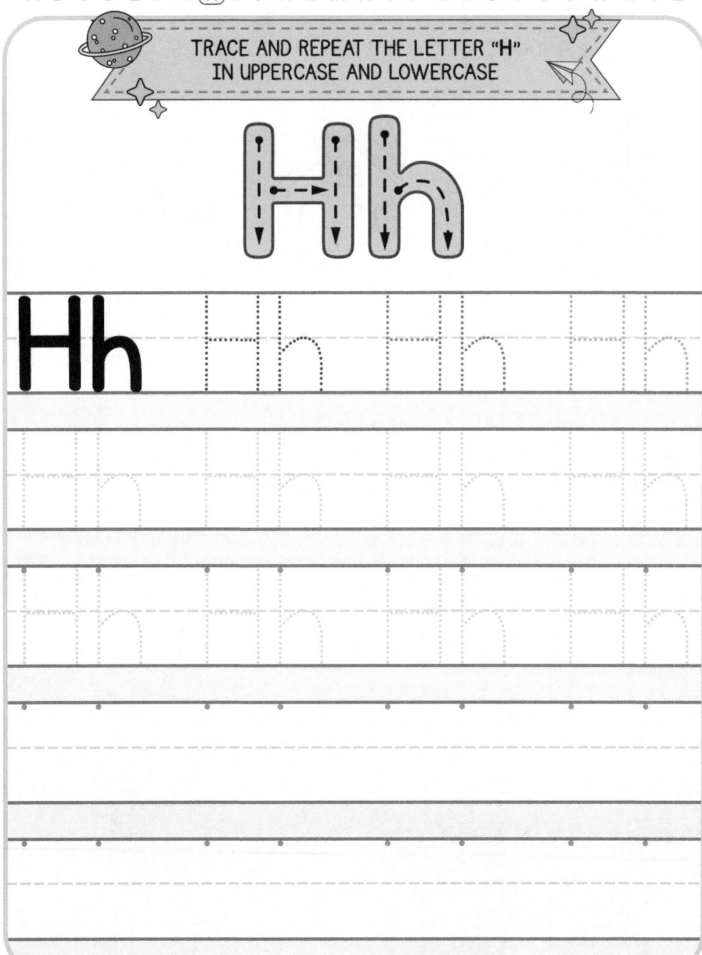

**TRACE AND REPEAT THE LETTER "H"
IN UPPERCASE AND LOWERCASE**

COMPLETE THIS SERIES OF ACTIVITIES
TO REINFORCE WHAT YOU HAVE LEARNED

1 Circle all the letters "H,h"

2 Color these things that are written with the letter "H,h"

Hand Hat

Hammer Horse

3 Complete the word with the missing letter

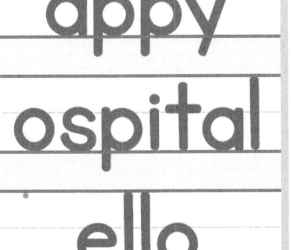

appy

ospital

ello

4 Draw something that begins or contains the letter "H,h"

TRACE AND THEN WRITE THE UPPERCASE LETTER "I" OF THE ALPHABET

Color me

"I" is for Island

SLAND

I

TRACE AND THEN WRITE THE LOWERCASE LETTER "i" OF THE ALPHABET

Color me

"I" is for Island

"Island" is "Isla" in Spanish

island

i

TRACE AND REPEAT THE LETTER "I"
IN UPPERCASE AND LOWERCASE

I i

COMPLETE THIS SERIES OF ACTIVITIES
TO REINFORCE WHAT YOU HAVE LEARNED

1 Circle all the letters "I, i"

2 Color these things that are written with the letter "I, i"

Ice cream

Igloo

Ink

Iguana

3 Complete the word with the missing letter

dea

mag ne

nsect

4 Draw something that begins or contains the letter "I, i"

TRACE AND THEN WRITE THE UPPERCASE LETTER "J" OF THE ALPHABET

Color me

"J" is for Jacket

JACKET

J J J J J J

TRACE AND THEN WRITE THE LOWERCASE LETTER "j" OF THE ALPHABET

j

Color me

"j" is for **jacket**

"Jacket" is "Chaqueta" in Spanish

jacket

j j j j j j

j j j j j j

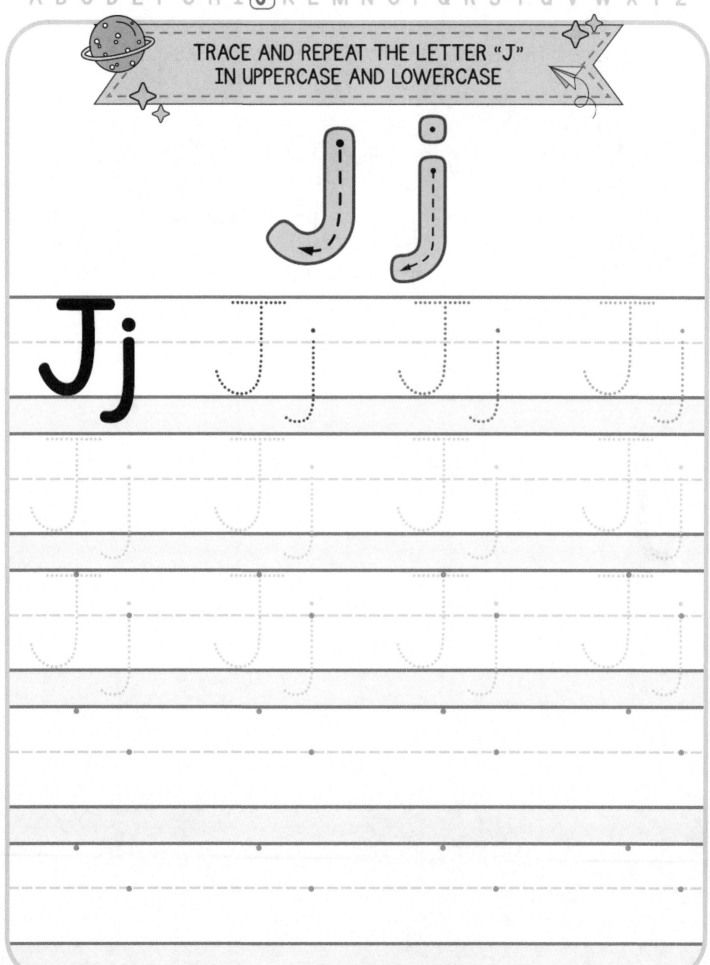

TRACE AND REPEAT THE LETTER "J"
IN UPPERCASE AND LOWERCASE

COMPLETE THIS SERIES OF ACTIVITIES
TO REINFORCE WHAT YOU HAVE LEARNED

1 Circle all the letters "Jj"

J D D a J o
T J
W R
V j
F j
j C A j
i J y

2 Color these things that are written with the letter "Jj"

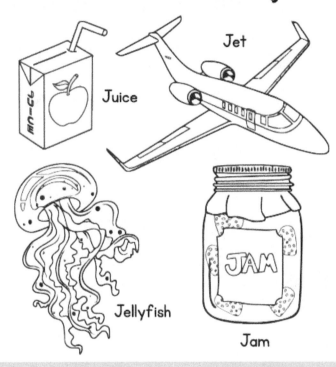

Jet

Juice

Jellyfish

JAM

Jam

3 Complete the word with the missing letter

ump

uly

ungle

4 Draw something that begins or contains the letter "Jj"

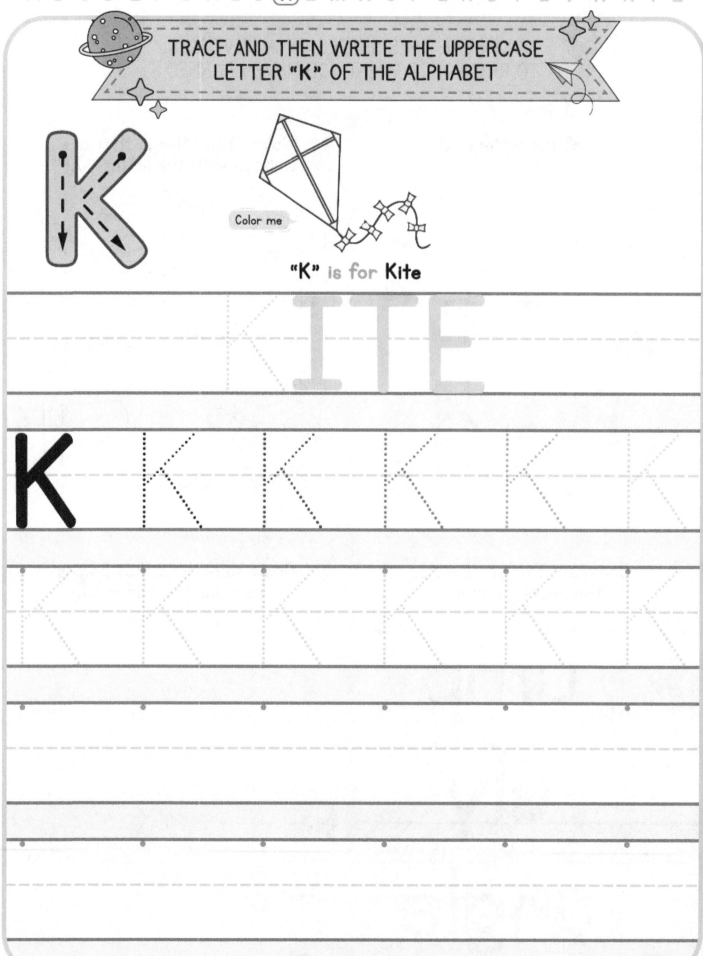

TRACE AND THEN WRITE THE UPPERCASE
LETTER "K" OF THE ALPHABET

Color me

"K" is for Kite

TRACE AND THEN WRITE THE LOWERCASE LETTER "k" OF THE ALPHABET

Color me

"k" is for **kite**

"Kite" is "Cometa" in Spanish

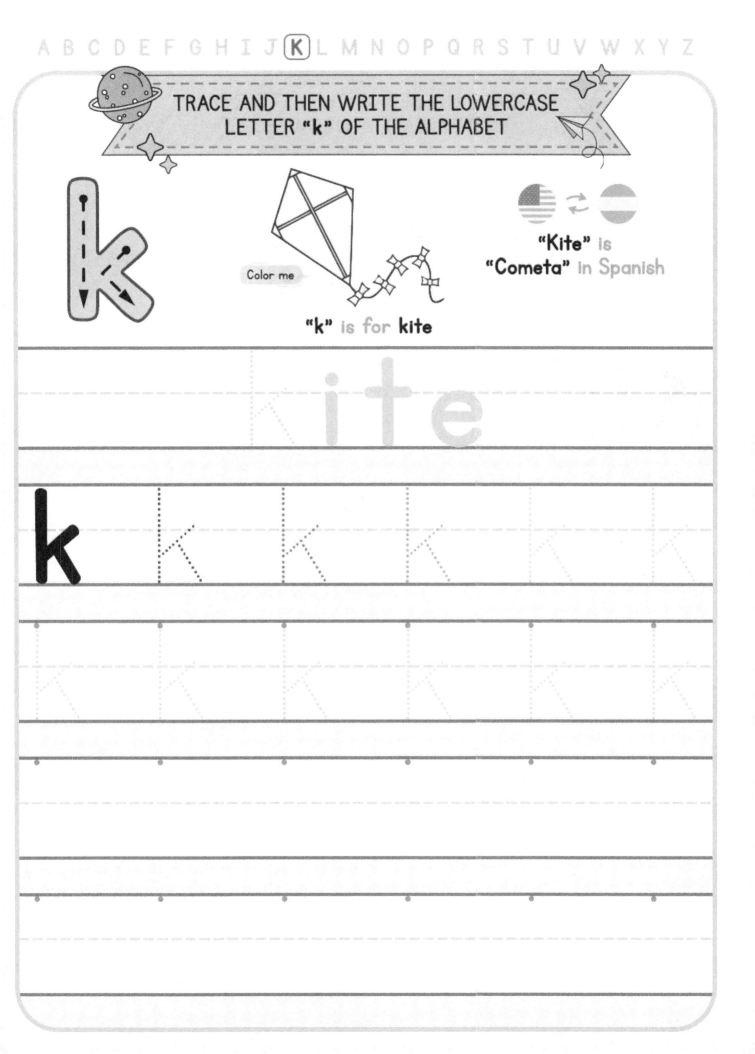

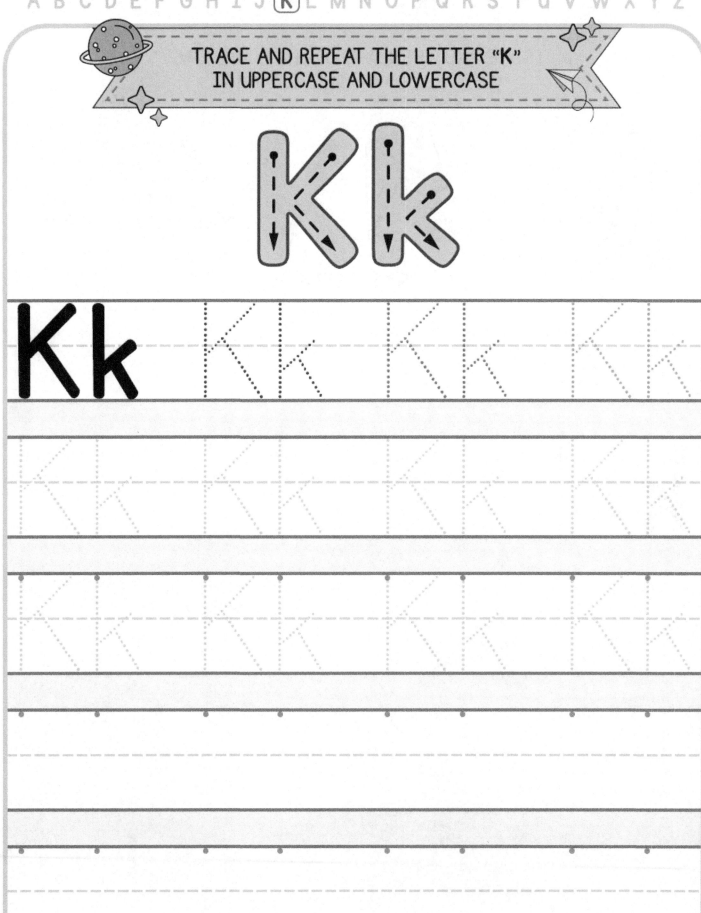

TRACE AND REPEAT THE LETTER "K"
IN UPPERCASE AND LOWERCASE

COMPLETE THIS SERIES OF ACTIVITIES
TO REINFORCE WHAT YOU HAVE LEARNED

1 Circle all the letters "K,k"

c R a K
K d R e
k k E a
d K
a k k V

2 Color these things that are written with the letter "K,k"

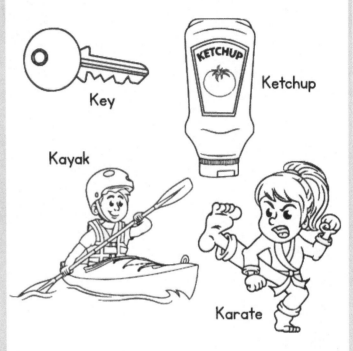

Key

KETCHUP
Ketchup

Kayak

Karate

3 Complete the word with the missing letter

iss

ic

itchen

4 Draw something that begins or contains the letter "K,k"

TRACE AND THEN WRITE THE UPPERCASE LETTER "L" OF THE ALPHABET

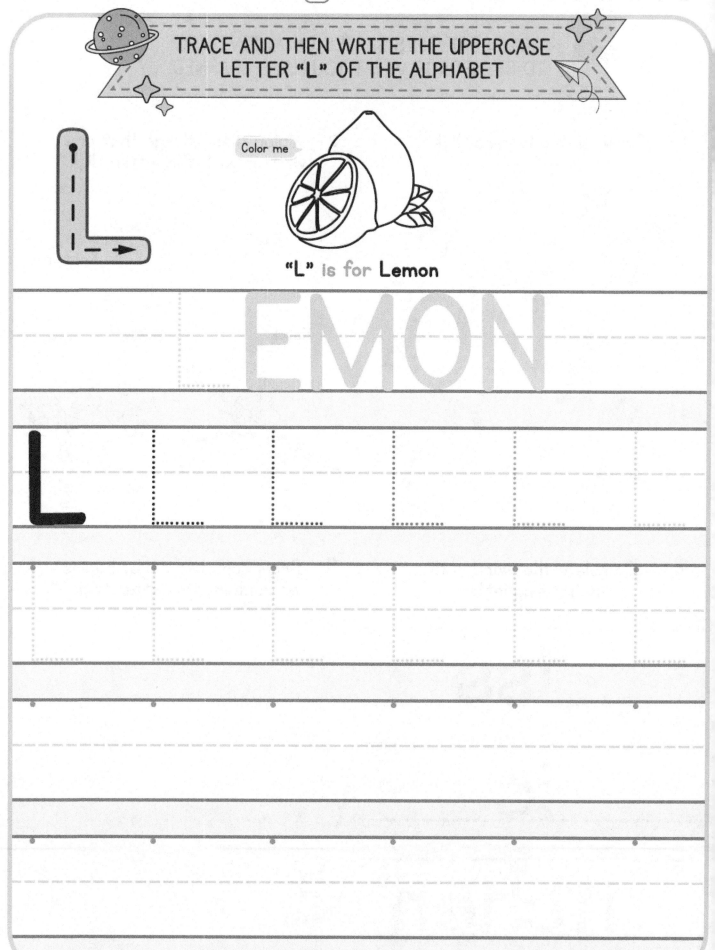

Color me

"L" is for Lemon

EMON

TRACE AND THEN WRITE THE LOWERCASE LETTER "l" OF THE ALPHABET

Color me

"l" is for **lemon**

"Lemon" is
"Limón" in Spanish

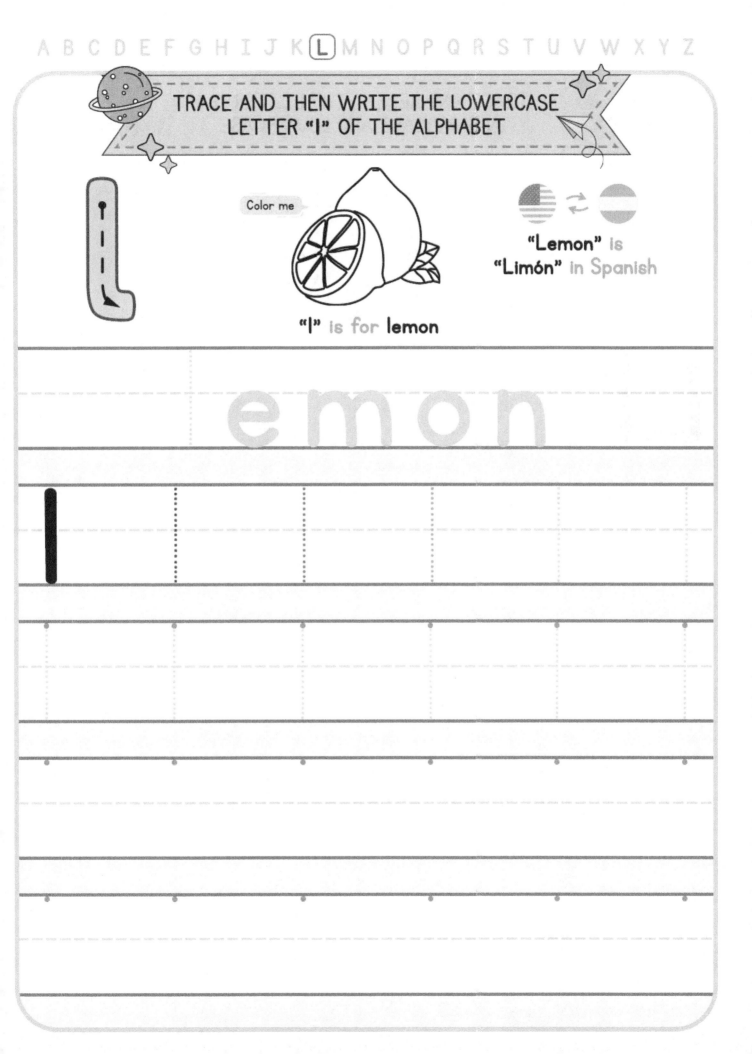

emon

TRACE AND REPEAT THE LETTER "L" IN UPPERCASE AND LOWERCASE

Ll

COMPLETE THIS SERIES OF ACTIVITIES TO REINFORCE WHAT YOU HAVE LEARNED

1 Circle all the letters "L,l"

2 Color these things that are written with the letter "L,l"

Lolly Pop

Lighthouse

Ladybug

Lion

3 Complete the word with the missing letter

ove

amp

unch

4 Draw something that begins or contains the letter "L,l"

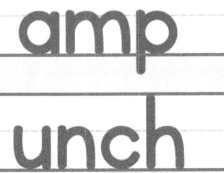

TRACE AND THEN WRITE THE UPPERCASE LETTER "M" OF THE ALPHABET

Color me

"M" is for **Monster**

ONSTER

M M M M M M M M

M M M M

TRACE AND THEN WRITE THE LOWERCASE LETTER "m" OF THE ALPHABET

m

Color me

"m" is for **monster**

"Monster" is "Monstruo" in Spanish

m m m m m m

m

TRACE AND REPEAT THE LETTER "M"
IN UPPERCASE AND LOWERCASE

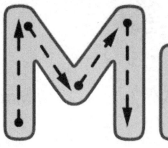 

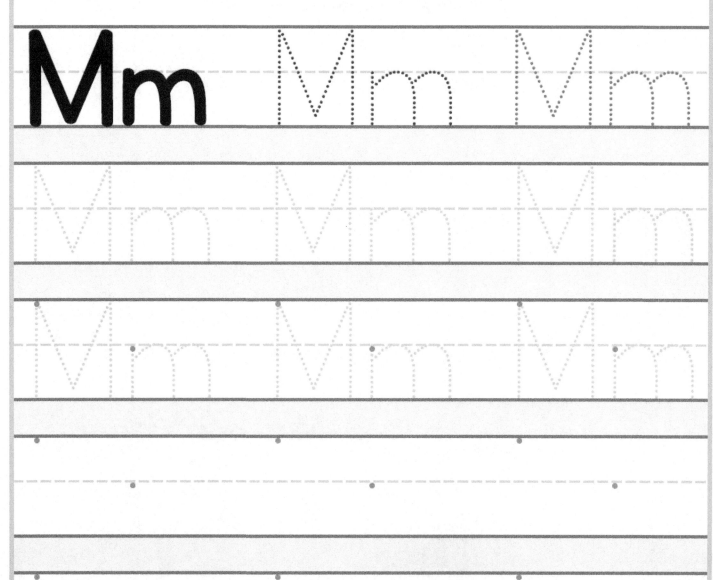

COMPLETE THIS SERIES OF ACTIVITIES
TO REINFORCE WHAT YOU HAVE LEARNED

1 Circle all the letters "**M,m**"

P A m a M
A d m a
m d M p F M
d m C w d

2 Color these things that are written with the letter "**M,m**"

Moon

Mouse

Mushroom

Monkey

3 Complete the word with the missing letter

ovie

achine

usic

4 Draw something that begins or contains the letter "**M,m**"

TRACE AND THEN WRITE THE UPPERCASE LETTER "N" OF THE ALPHABET

Color me

"N" is for Nurse

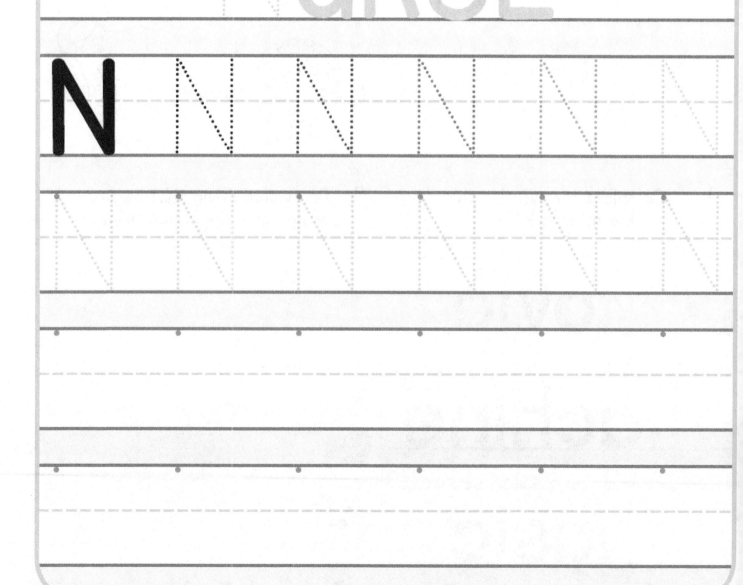

TRACE AND THEN WRITE THE LOWERCASE LETTER "n" OF THE ALPHABET

Color me

"n" is for **nurse**

"Nurse" is
"Enfermera" in Spanish

n u r s e

n n n n n n

TRACE AND REPEAT THE LETTER "N" IN UPPERCASE AND LOWERCASE

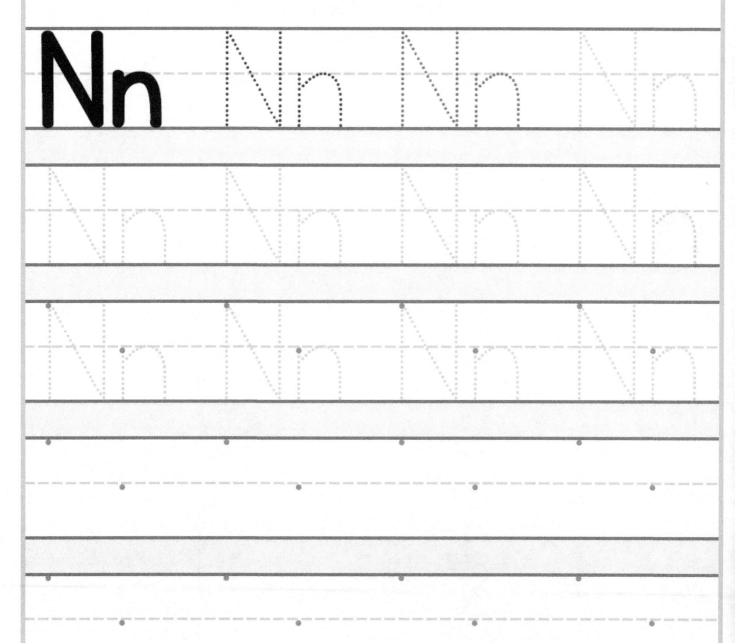

COMPLETE THIS SERIES OF ACTIVITIES
TO REINFORCE WHAT YOU HAVE LEARNED

1 Circle all the letters "N,n"

M N a n
A n J e
n H
T E N S
N e n V
N

2 Color these things that are
written with the letter "N,n"

Nail   Numbers

Net

Ninja

3 Complete the word with
the missing letter

ight

ose

otebook

4 Draw something that begins
or contains the letter "N,n"

TRACE AND THEN WRITE THE UPPERCASE LETTER "O" OF THE ALPHABET

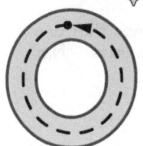

Color me

"O" is for Orange

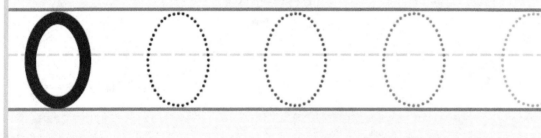

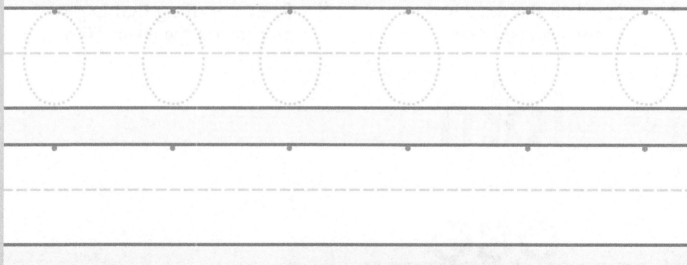

TRACE AND THEN WRITE THE LOWERCASE LETTER "o" OF THE ALPHABET

Color me

"o" is for **orange**

"Orange" is "Naranja" in Spanish

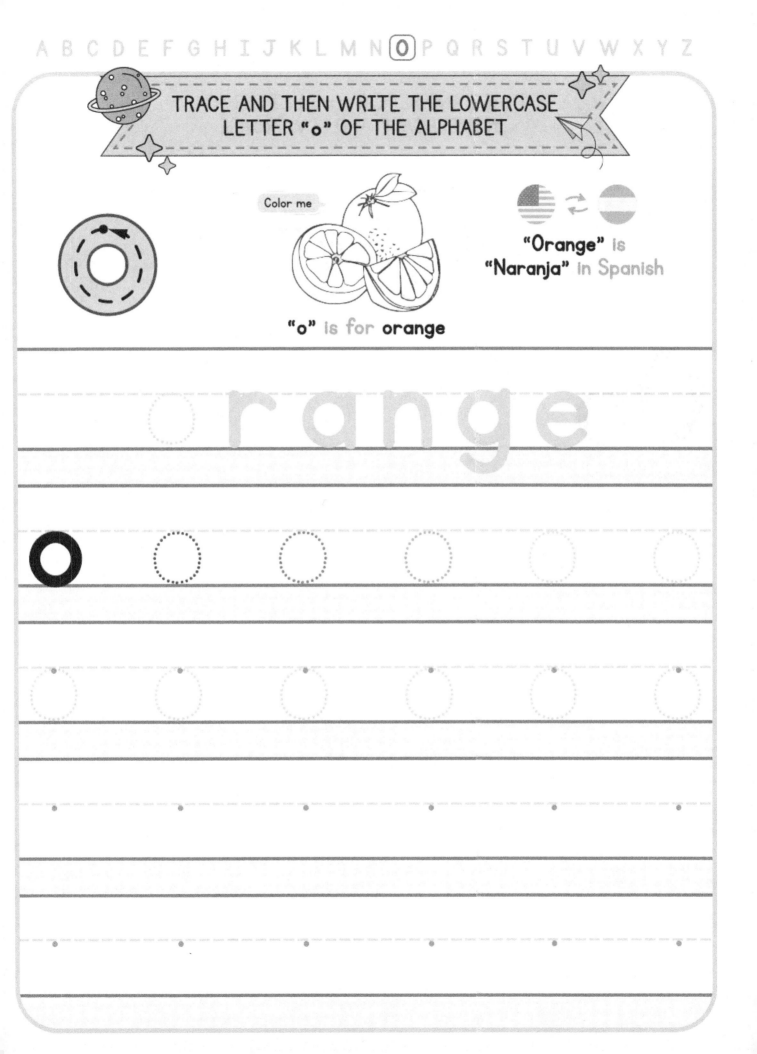

TRACE AND REPEAT THE LETTER "O" IN UPPERCASE AND LOWERCASE

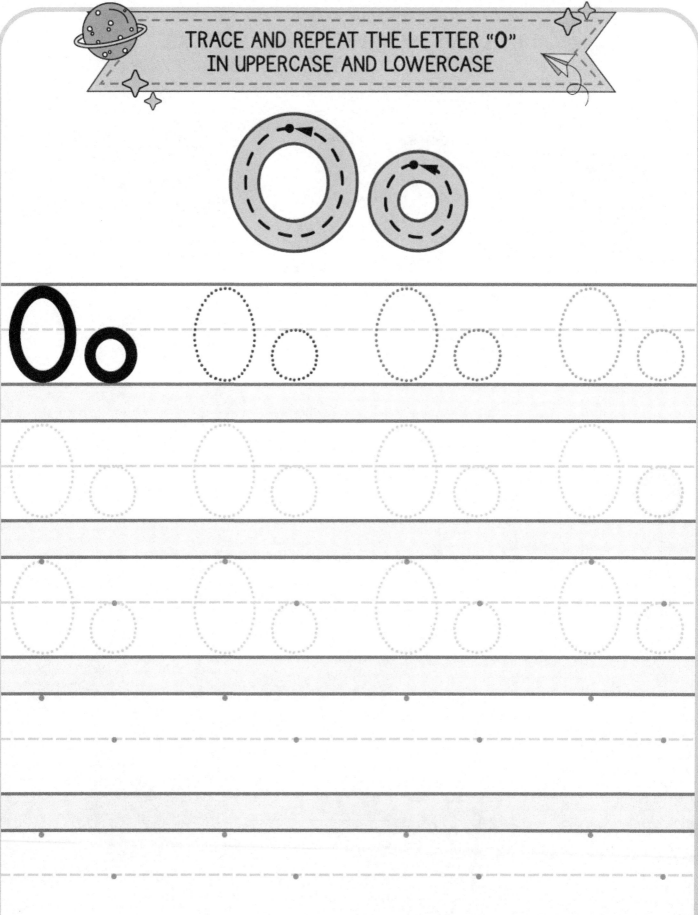

COMPLETE THIS SERIES OF ACTIVITIES
TO REINFORCE WHAT YOU HAVE LEARNED

1 Circle all the letters "O,o"

2 Color these things that are written with the letter "O,o"

Oars

Onion

Ostrich

Oven

3 Complete the word with the missing letter

cean

ffice

ld

4 Draw something that begins or contains the letter "O,o"

TRACE AND THEN WRITE THE UPPERCASE
LETTER "P" OF THE ALPHABET

Color me

"P" is for Pig

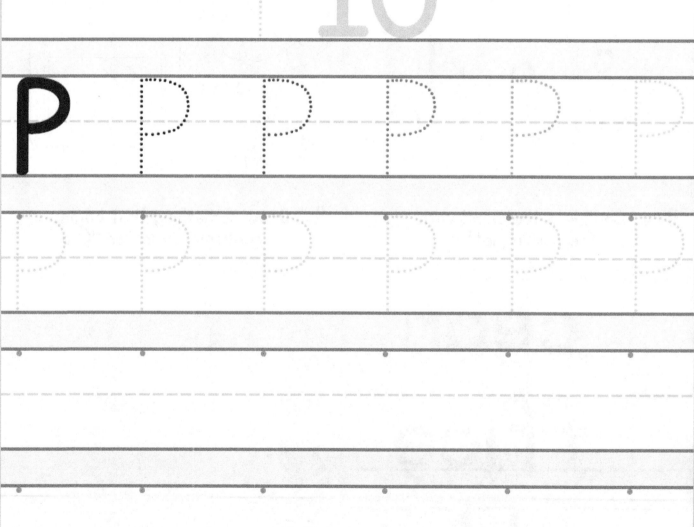

TRACE AND THEN WRITE THE LOWERCASE LETTER "p" OF THE ALPHABET

p

Color me

"p" is for pig

"Pig" is "Cerdo" in Spanish

ig

p   p   p   p   p   p   p

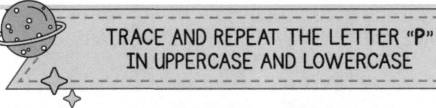

TRACE AND REPEAT THE LETTER "P"
IN UPPERCASE AND LOWERCASE

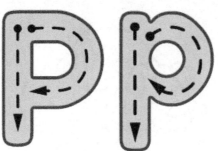

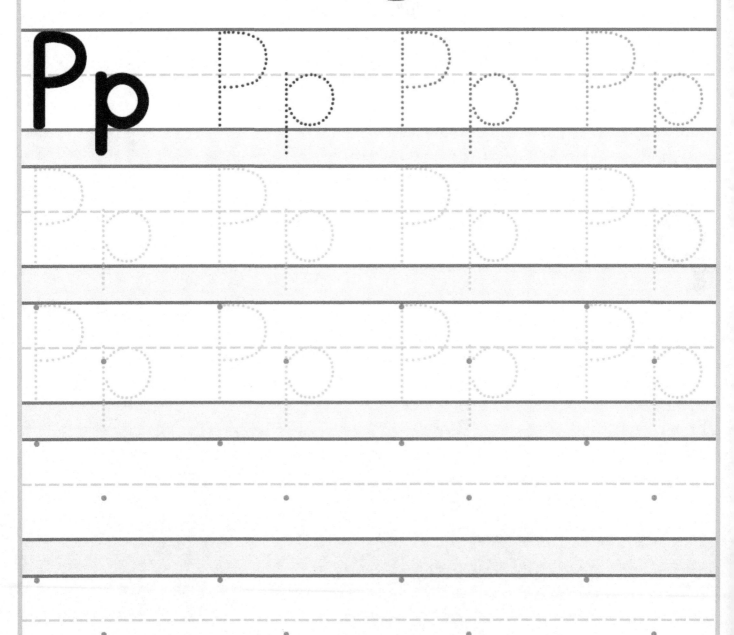

Pp

TRACE AND REPEAT THE LETTER "P"

COMPLETE THIS SERIES OF ACTIVITIES
TO REINFORCE WHAT YOU HAVE LEARNED

1 Circle all the letters "P,p"

2 Color these things that are written with the letter "P,p"

Pizza

Popcorn

POP CORN

Piano

Pineapple

3 Complete the word with the missing letter

lace

ark

arty

4 Draw something that begins or contains the letter "P,p"

TRACE AND THEN WRITE THE UPPERCASE LETTER "Q" OF THE ALPHABET

Color me

"Q" is for Queen

TRACE AND THEN WRITE THE LOWERCASE LETTER "q" OF THE ALPHABET

Color me

"q" is for **queen**

"Queen" is "Reina" in Spanish

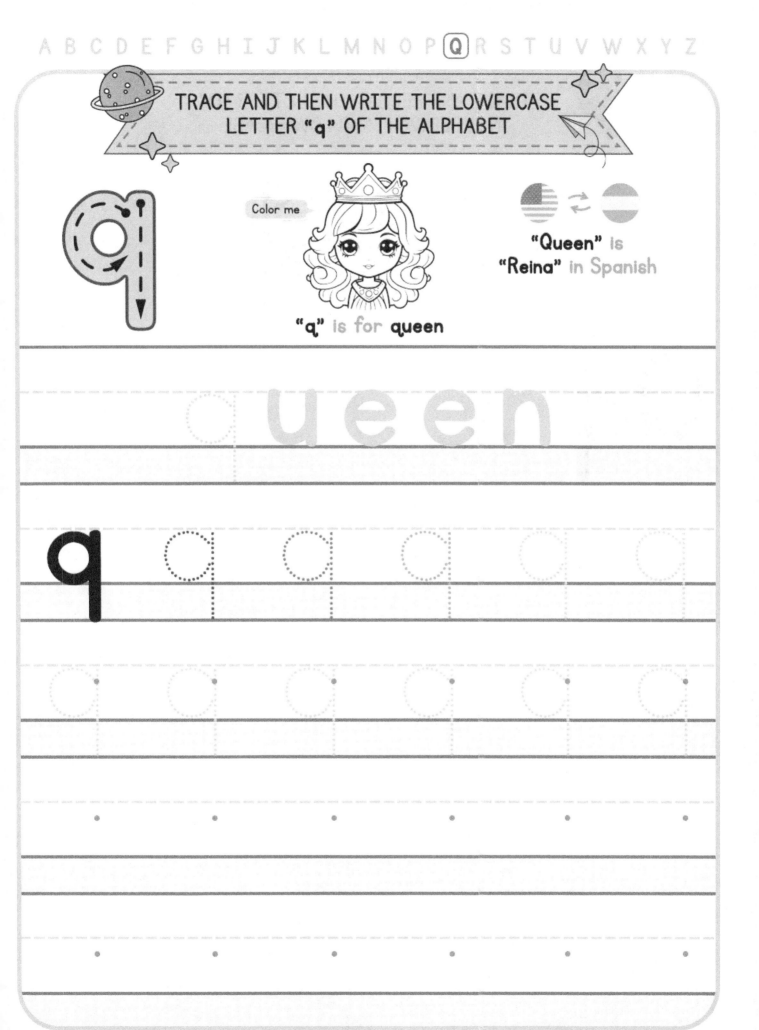

queen

q q q q q q

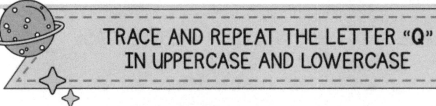

TRACE AND REPEAT THE LETTER "Q" IN UPPERCASE AND LOWERCASE

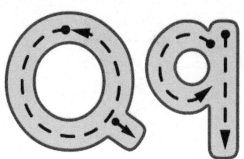

Qq

COMPLETE THIS SERIES OF ACTIVITIES TO REINFORCE WHAT YOU HAVE LEARNED

1 Circle all the letters "Q,q"

Q R a B
D Q R e
q j f Q
d S
e Q w q

2 Color these things that are written with the letter "Q,q"

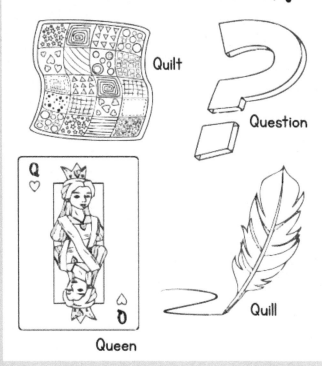

Quilt

Question

Queen

Quill

3 Complete the word with the missing letter

uick

uiet

uiz

4 Draw something that begins or contains the letter "Q,q"

TRACE AND THEN WRITE THE UPPERCASE LETTER "R" OF THE ALPHABET

Color me

"R" is for Rabbit

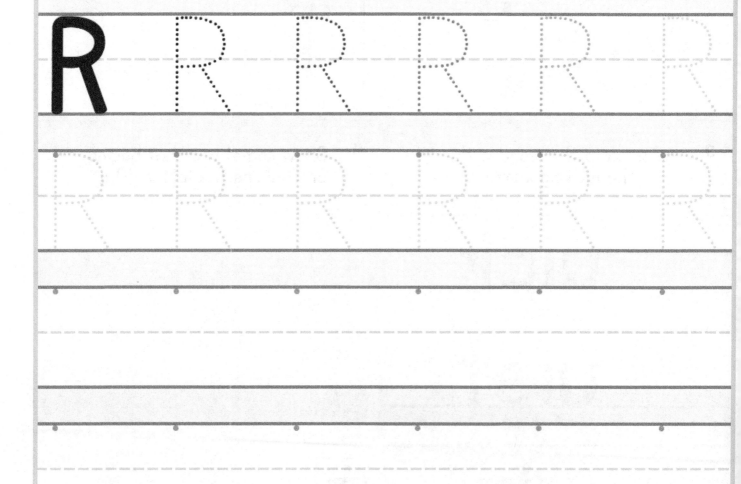

TRACE AND THEN WRITE THE LOWERCASE LETTER "r" OF THE ALPHABET

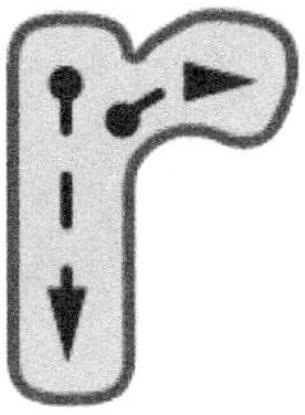

Color me

"r" is for **rabbit**

"Rabbit" is "Conejo" in Spanish

r

r a b b i t

r r r r r r

r r r r r r r

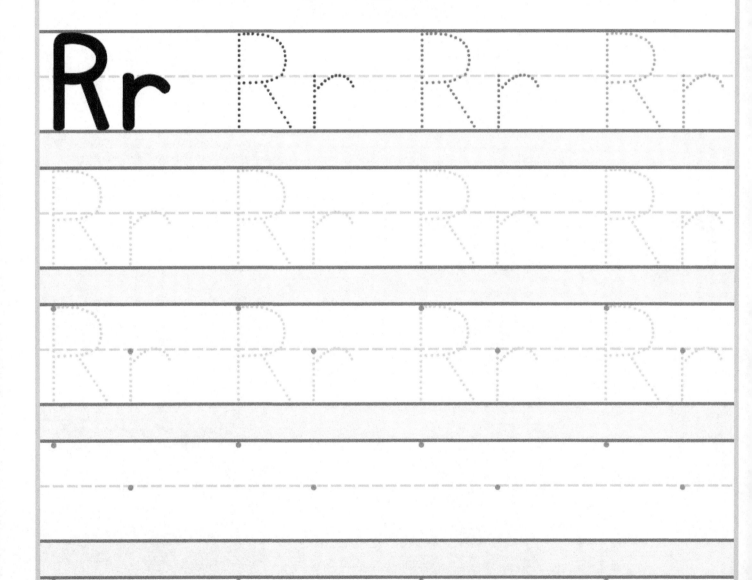

COMPLETE THIS SERIES OF ACTIVITIES TO REINFORCE WHAT YOU HAVE LEARNED

1 Circle all the letters "R,r"

2 Color these things that are written with the letter "R,r"

Rooster

Rose

Robot

Rocket

3 Complete the word with the missing letter

ain

ive

oom

4 Draw something that begins or contains the letter "R,r"

A B C D E F G H I J K L M N O P Q R (S) T U V W X Y Z

TRACE AND THEN WRITE THE UPPERCASE LETTER "S" OF THE ALPHABET

Color me

"S" is for Shoes

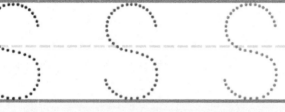

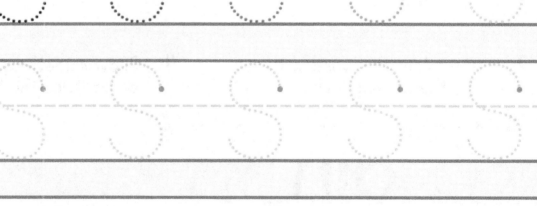

TRACE AND THEN WRITE THE LOWERCASE LETTER "s" OF THE ALPHABET

Color me

"s" is for **shoes**

"Shoes" is
"Zapatos" in Spanish

s h o e s

s   s   s   s   s   s

s   s   s   s   s   s

s   s   s   s   s   s

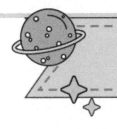
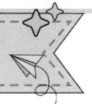

TRACE AND REPEAT THE LETTER "S"
IN UPPERCASE AND LOWERCASE

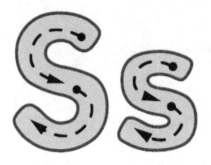

Ss

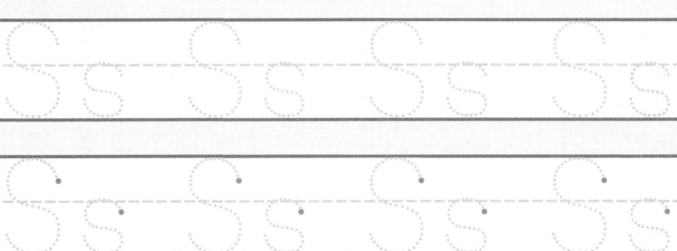

COMPLETE THIS SERIES OF ACTIVITIES
TO REINFORCE WHAT YOU HAVE LEARNED

1 Circle all the letters "S,s"

S A a B
k S R S
d L G
s A s
N e s S
S V

2 Color these things that are written with the letter "S,s"

Shark

Submarine

Snake

Strawberry

3 Complete the word with the missing letter

i ter

and

mile

4 Draw something that begins or contains the letter "S,s"

TRACE AND THEN WRITE THE UPPERCASE LETTER "T" OF THE ALPHABET

Color me

"T" is for **Tomato**

OMA   O

T

TRACE AND THEN WRITE THE LOWERCASE LETTER "t" OF THE ALPHABET

Color me

"t" is for **tomato**

"Tomato" is
"Tomate" in Spanish

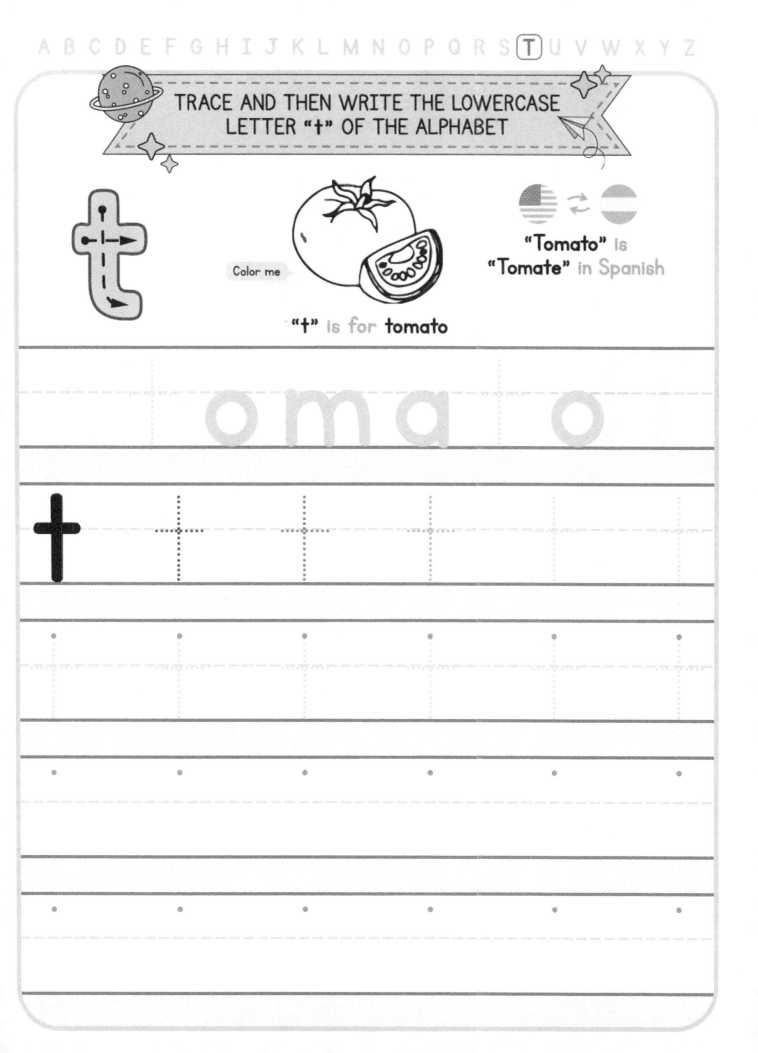

A B C D E F G H I J K L M N O P Q R S (T) U V W X Y Z

TRACE AND REPEAT THE LETTER "T"
IN UPPERCASE AND LOWERCASE

T t

Tt

COMPLETE THIS SERIES OF ACTIVITIES
TO REINFORCE WHAT YOU HAVE LEARNED

1 Circle all the letters "T,t"

2 Color these things that are written with the letter "T,t"

Tree

Tuba

Tools

Turtle

3 Complete the word with the missing letter

oday

eacher

ime

4 Draw something that begins or contains the letter "T,t"

TRACE AND THEN WRITE THE UPPERCASE LETTER "U" OF THE ALPHABET

Color me

"U" is for Unicorn

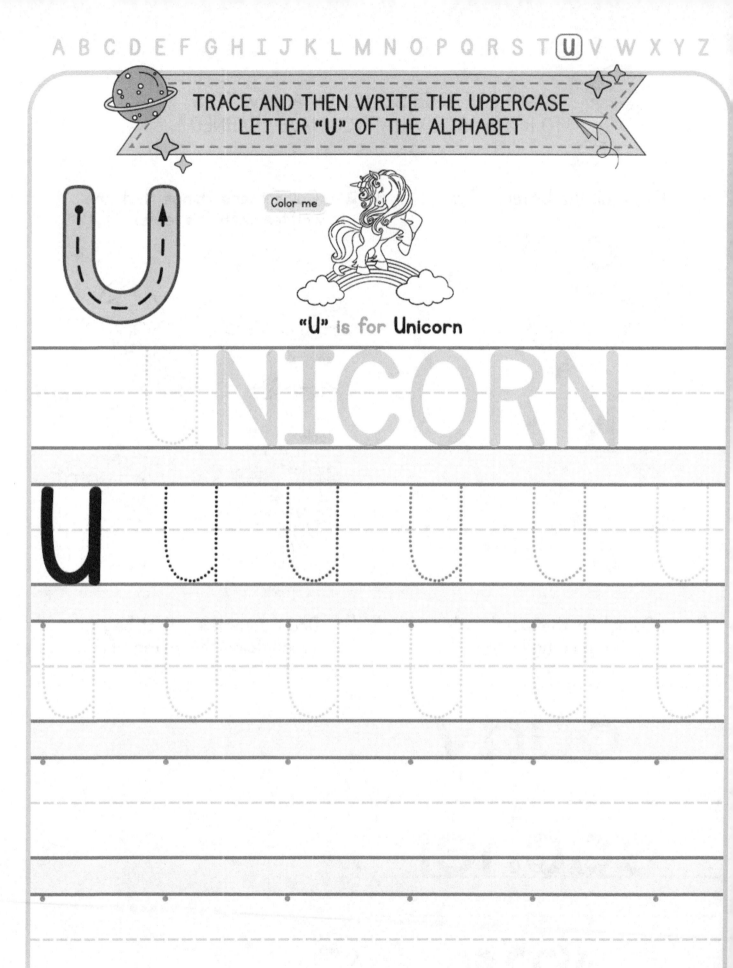

UNICORN

TRACE AND THEN WRITE THE LOWERCASE LETTER "u" OF THE ALPHABET

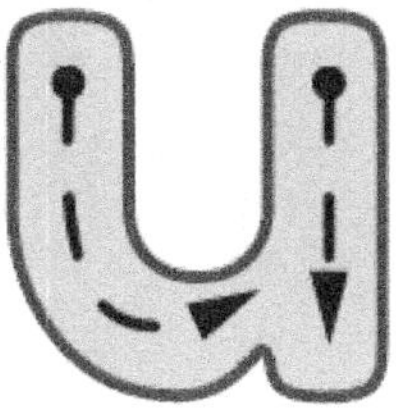

Color me

"u" is for **unicorn**

"Unicorn" is "Unicornio" in Spanish

unicorn

u

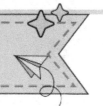

TRACE AND REPEAT THE LETTER "U" IN UPPERCASE AND LOWERCASE

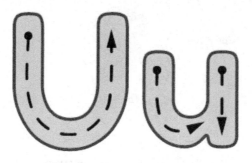

Uu

COMPLETE THIS SERIES OF ACTIVITIES TO REINFORCE WHAT YOU HAVE LEARNED

1 Circle all the letters "U,u"

E U U a u
G a u V
g U L u
x U P
U A J V
A u

2 Color these things that are written with the letter "U,u"

Uniform
PLAYER 17
Umbrella
Urn
Unicycle

3 Complete the word with the missing letter

ncle

niverse

gly

4 Draw something that begins or contains the letter "U,u"

TRACE AND THEN WRITE THE UPPERCASE LETTER "V" OF THE ALPHABET

Color me

"V" is for **Vulture**

TRACE AND THEN WRITE THE LOWERCASE LETTER "v" OF THE ALPHABET

Color me

"v" is for vulture

"Vulture" is "Buitre" in Spanish

vulture

v v v v v v v

TRACE AND REPEAT THE LETTER "V" IN UPPERCASE AND LOWERCASE

Vv

COMPLETE THIS SERIES OF ACTIVITIES TO REINFORCE WHAT YOU HAVE LEARNED

1 Circle all the letters "V,v"

2 Color these things that are written with the letter "V,v"

Vampire

Vacuum cleaner

a e i o u
Vowels

Violin

3 Complete the word with the missing letter

illage

ictory

acation

4 Draw something that begins or contains the letter "V,v"

TRACE AND THEN WRITE THE UPPERCASE LETTER "W" OF THE ALPHABET

Color me

"W" is for Whale

W HALE

W W W W W W W

TRACE AND THEN WRITE THE LOWERCASE
LETTER "w" OF THE ALPHABET

Color me

"w" is for whale

"Whale" is
"Ballena" in Spanish

whale

w   w   w   w   w

w   w   w   w

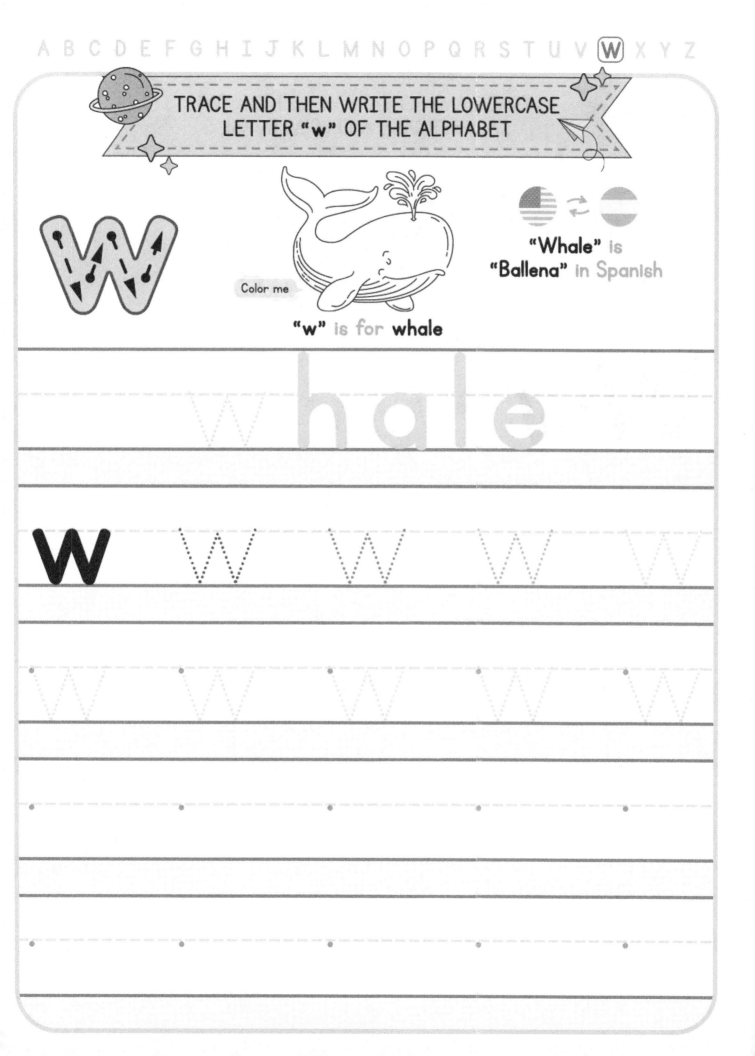

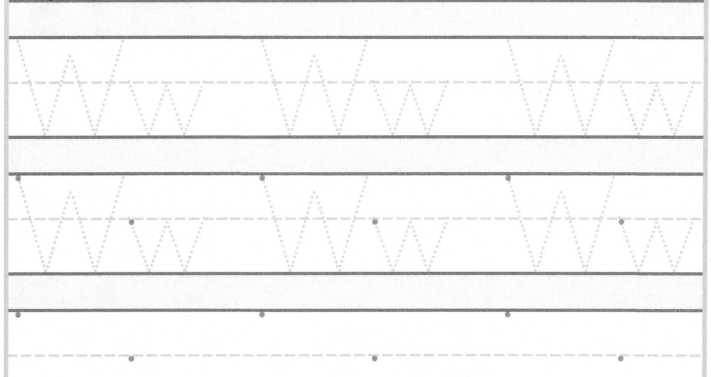

COMPLETE THIS SERIES OF ACTIVITIES
TO REINFORCE WHAT YOU HAVE LEARNED

1 Circle all the letters "**W,w**"

O R W B
w A w e
f d W a d W
s W C d j
w

2 Color these things that are written with the letter "**W,w**"

Wizard

Water boots

Wheelbarrow

Witch

3 Complete the word with the missing letter

inter

oman

orld

4 Draw something that begins or contains the letter "**W,w**"

TRACE AND THEN WRITE THE UPPERCASE LETTER "X" OF THE ALPHABET

Color me

"X" is for **Xylophone**

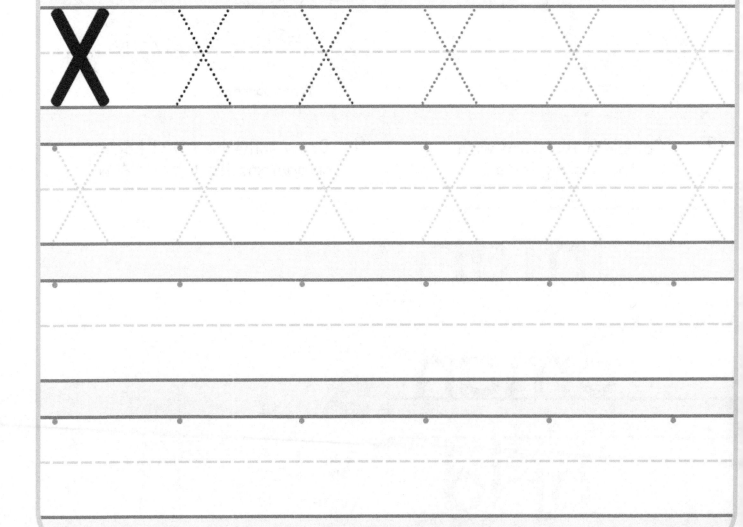

TRACE AND THEN WRITE THE LOWERCASE LETTER "x" OF THE ALPHABET

Color me

"x" is for xylophone

"Xylophone" is "Xilófono" in Spanish

x ylophone

x   x   x   x   x   x

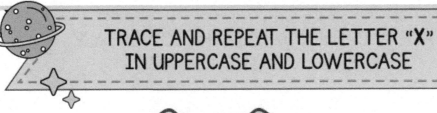

TRACE AND REPEAT THE LETTER "X" IN UPPERCASE AND LOWERCASE

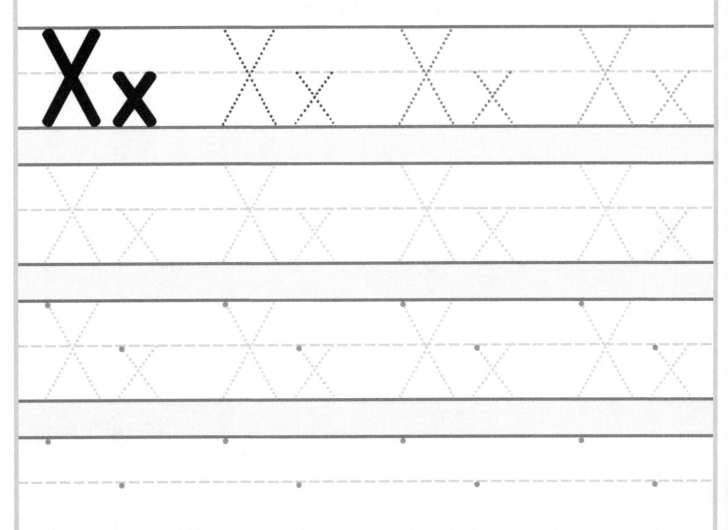

COMPLETE THIS SERIES OF ACTIVITIES TO REINFORCE WHAT YOU HAVE LEARNED

1 Circle all the letters "X,x"

2 Color these things that are written with the letter "X,x"

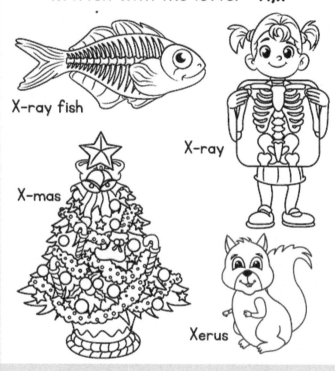

X-ray fish

X-ray

X-mas

Xerus

3 Complete the word with the missing letter

Ta_i

Ne_t

Fi_

4 Draw something that begins or contains the letter "X,x"

TRACE AND THEN WRITE THE UPPERCASE LETTER "Y" OF THE ALPHABET

Color me

"Y" is for Yarn

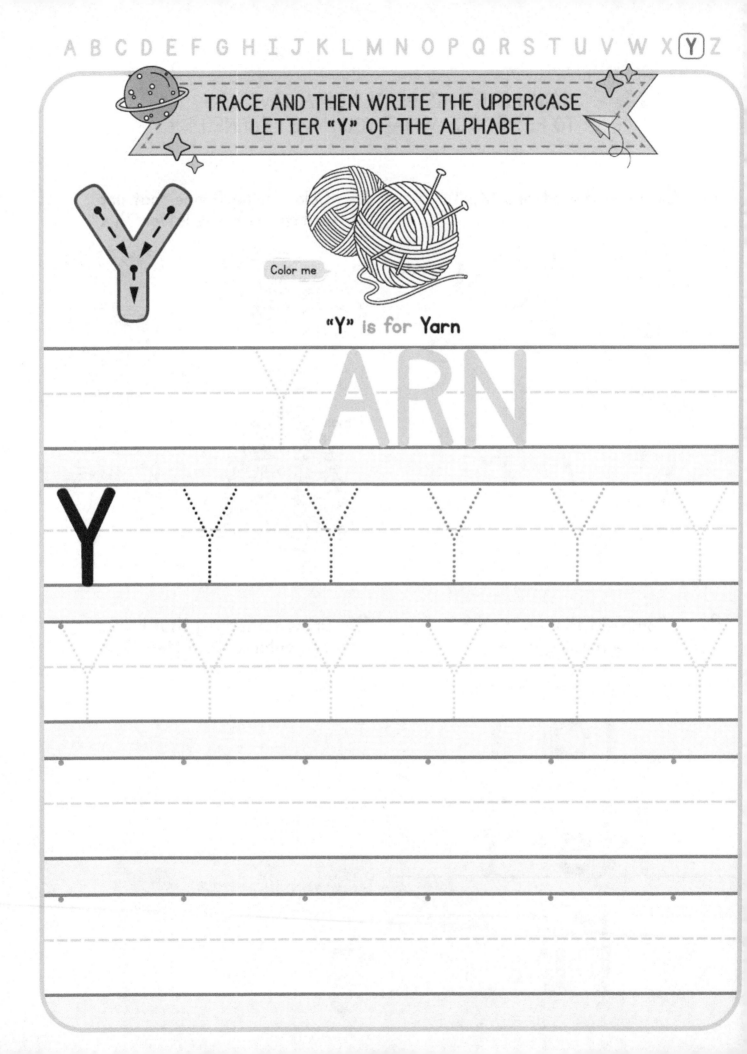

TRACE AND THEN WRITE THE LOWERCASE LETTER "y" OF THE ALPHABET

Color me

"y" is for **yarn**

"Yarn" is "Hilo" in Spanish

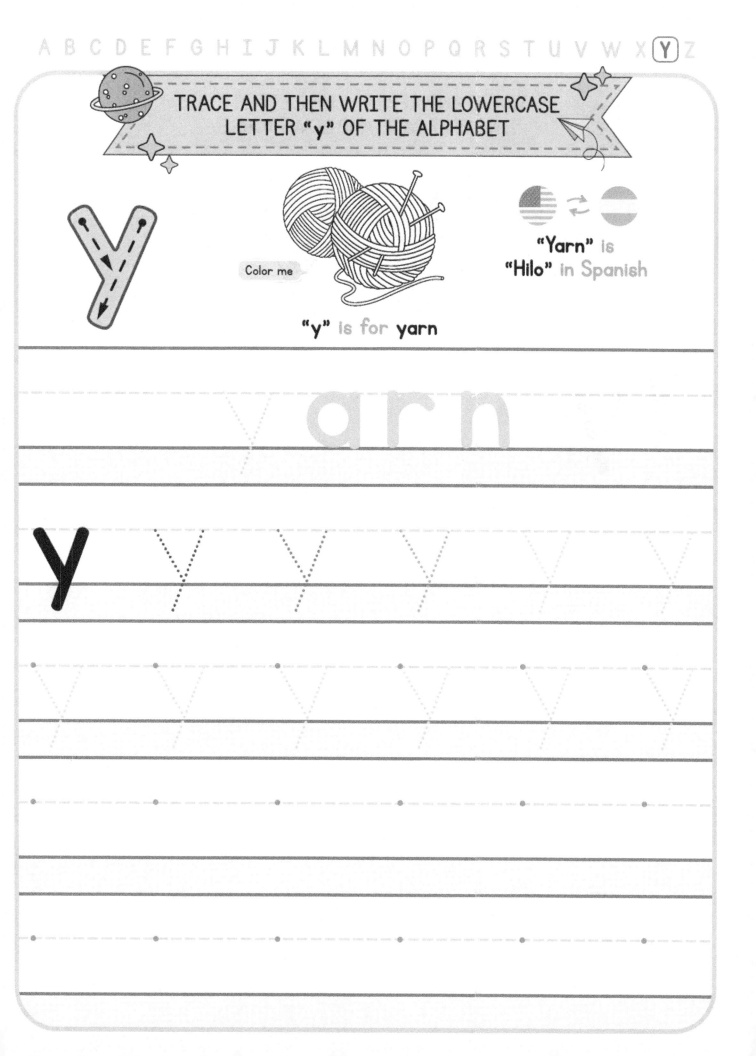

y arn

y y y y y y

TRACE AND REPEAT THE LETTER "Y"
IN UPPERCASE AND LOWERCASE

Y y

Yy

1 Circle all the letters "Y,y"

2 Color these things that are written with the letter "Y,y"

Yak

Yelk

Yoga

Yo-Yo

3 Complete the word with the missing letter

ellow

es

ear

4 Draw something that begins or contains the letter "Y,y"

TRACE AND THEN WRITE THE UPPERCASE LETTER "Z" OF THE ALPHABET

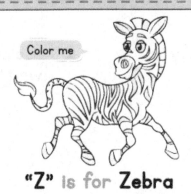

Color me

"Z" is for Zebra

ZEBRA

Z

TRACE AND THEN WRITE THE LOWERCASE LETTER "z" OF THE ALPHABET

Color me

"z" is for **zebra**

"Zebra" is
"Cebra" in Spanish

z ebra

z z z z z

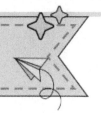

TRACE AND REPEAT THE LETTER "Z"
IN UPPERCASE AND LOWERCASE

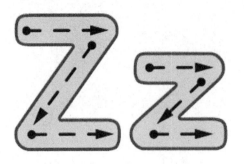

Zz

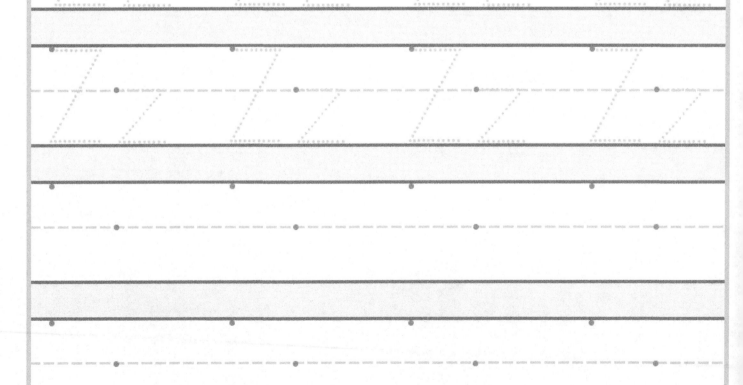

 COMPLETE THIS SERIES OF ACTIVITIES
TO REINFORCE WHAT YOU HAVE LEARNED

1 Circle all the letters "Z,z"

P Z a z
r S Z
Z R e
P Z Z m
e d z C L z
z Z V

2 Color these things that are written with the letter "Z,z"

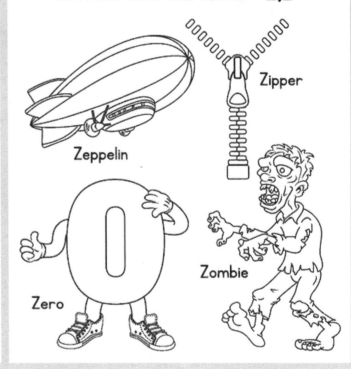

Zeppelin

Zipper

Zero

Zombie

3 Complete the word with the missing letter

one

odiac

oo

4 Draw something that begins or contains the letter "Z,z"

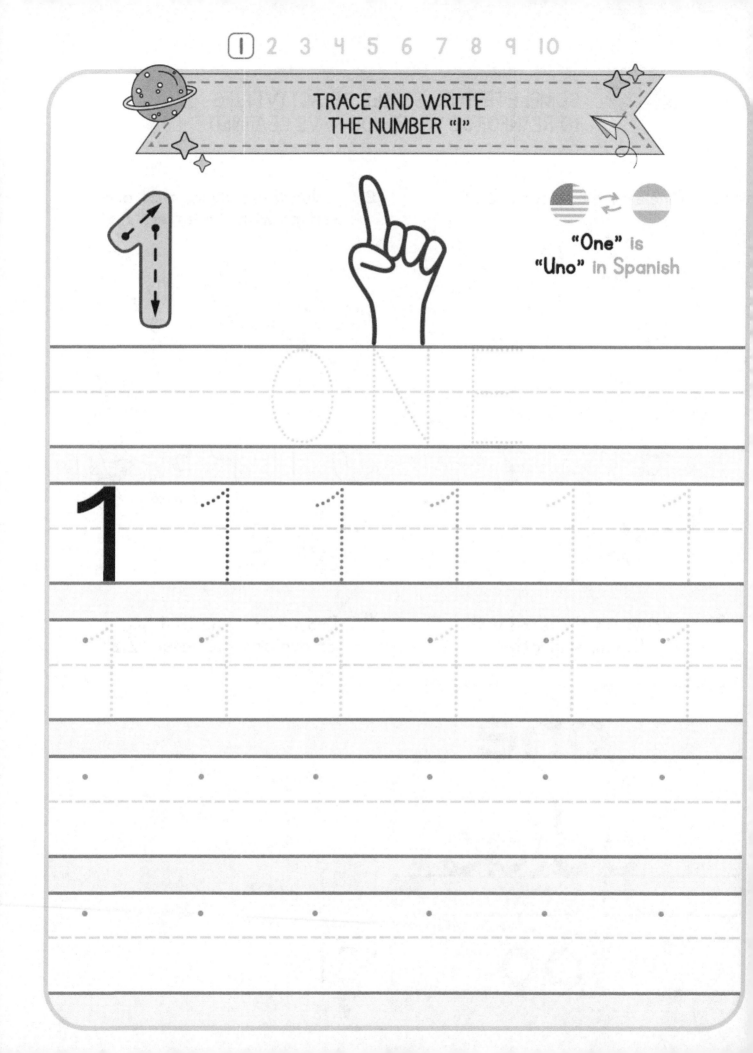

TRACE AND WRITE
THE NUMBER "1"

"One" is
"Uno" in Spanish

TRACE AND WRITE
THE NUMBER "2"

"Two" is
"Dos" in Spanish

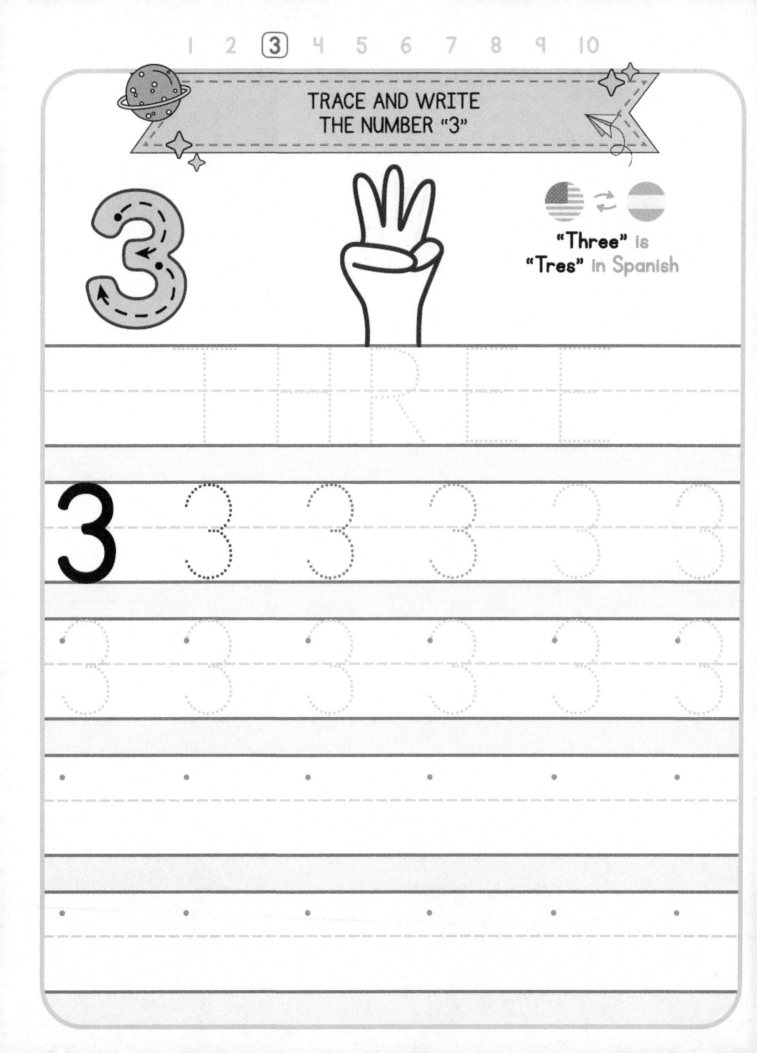

TRACE AND WRITE
THE NUMBER "3"

"Three" is "Tres" in Spanish

TRACE AND WRITE
THE NUMBER "4"

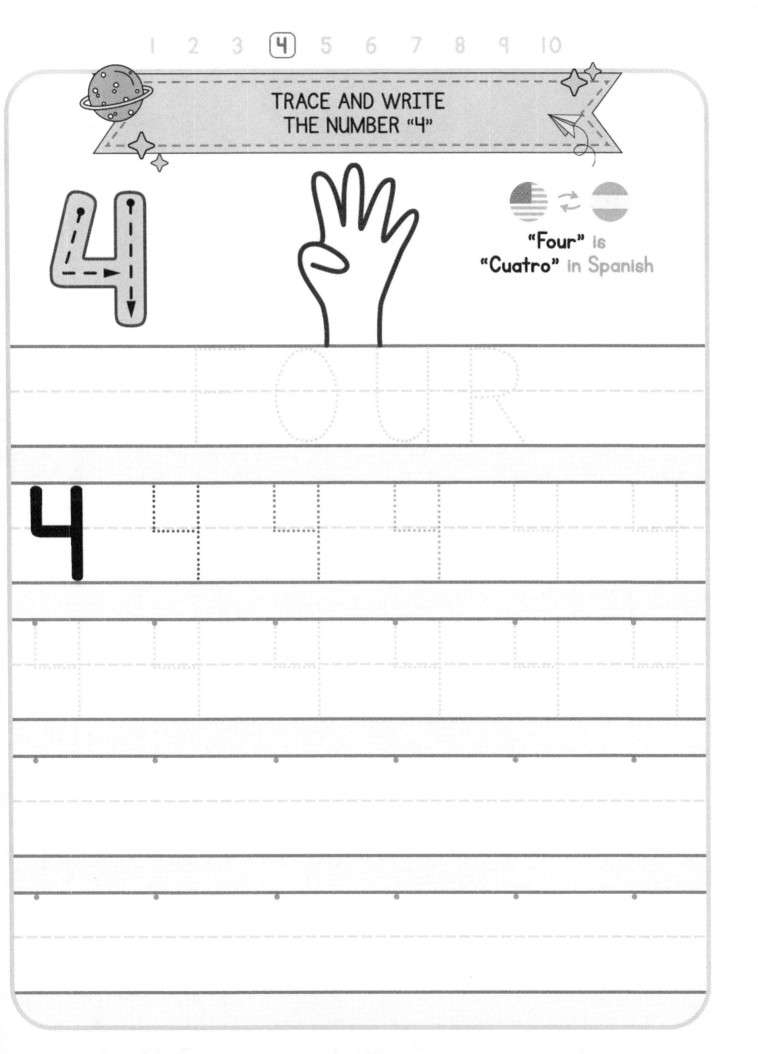

"Four" is
"Cuatro" in Spanish

TRACE AND WRITE
THE NUMBER "5"

"Five" is
"Cinco" in Spanish

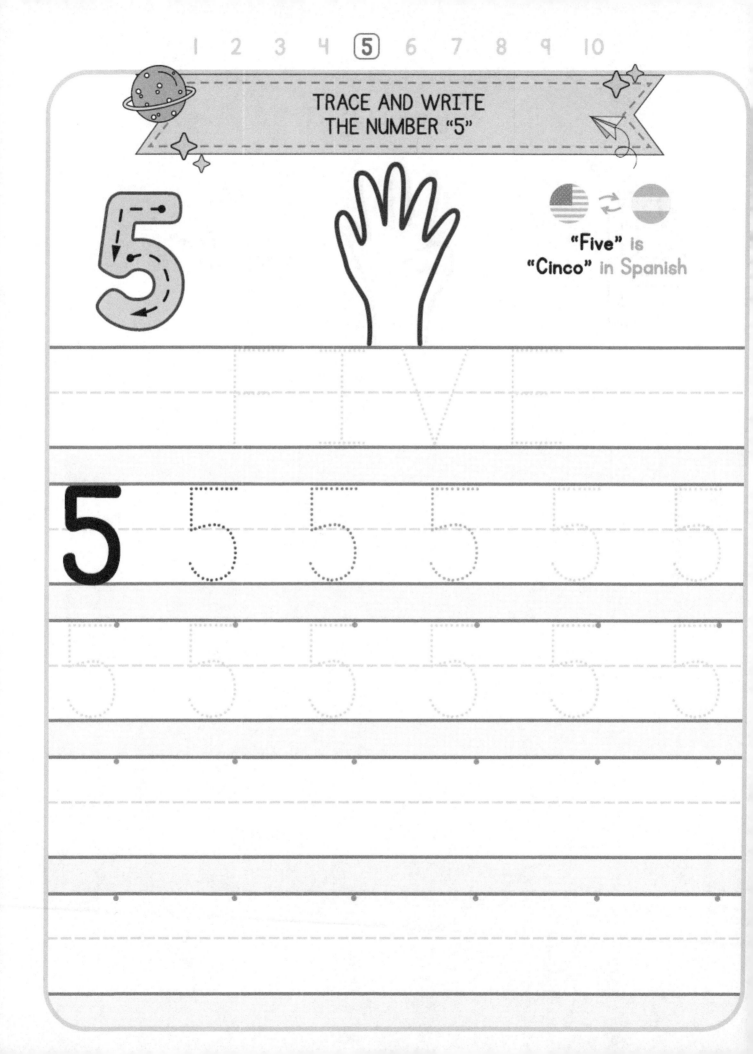

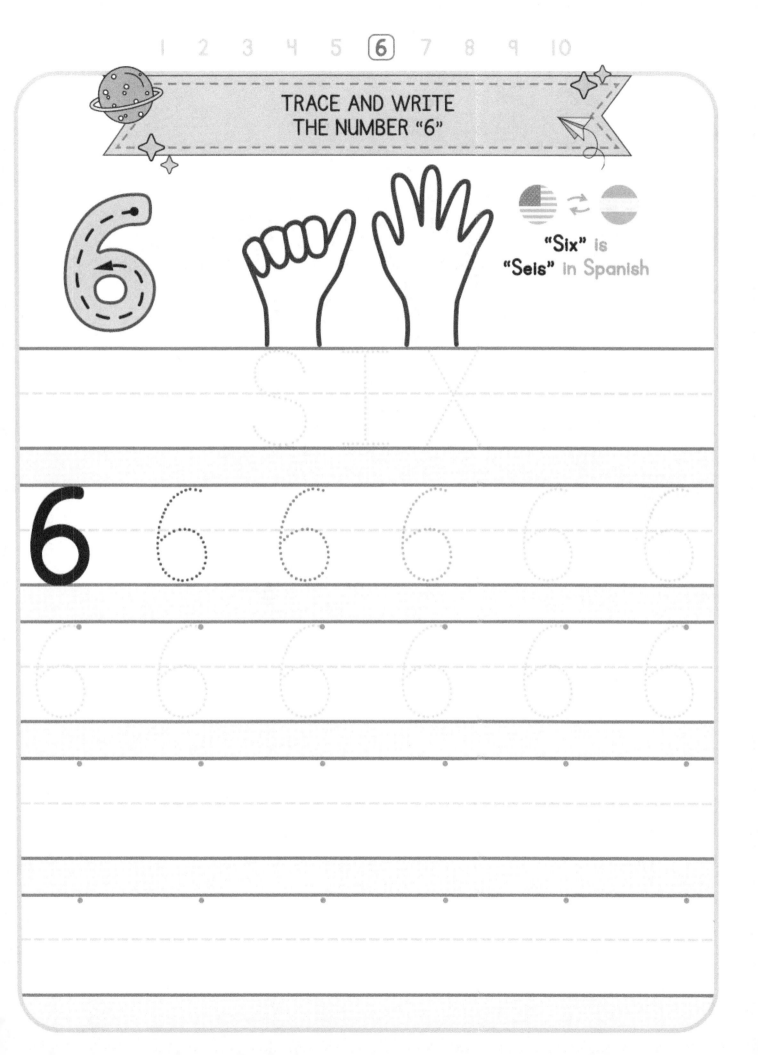

TRACE AND WRITE
THE NUMBER "6"

"Six" is
"Seis" in Spanish

TRACE AND WRITE
THE NUMBER "7"

"Seven" is
"Siete" in Spanish

7

SEVEN

TRACE AND WRITE
THE NUMBER "8"

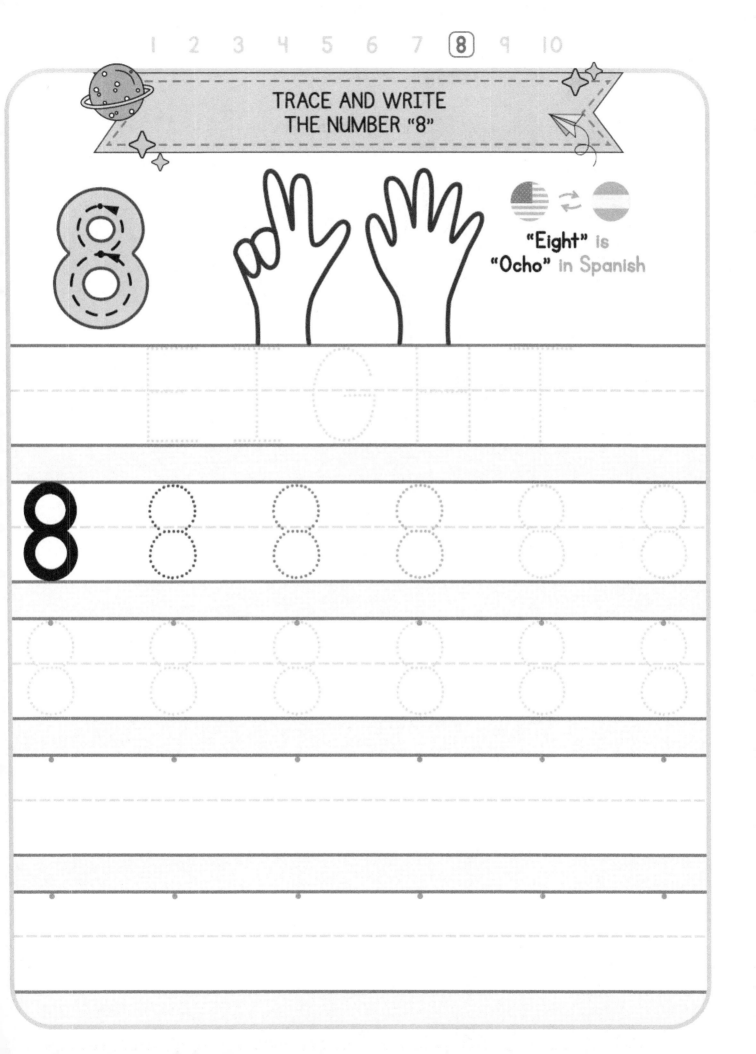

"Eight" is
"Ocho" in Spanish

TRACE AND WRITE
THE NUMBER "9"

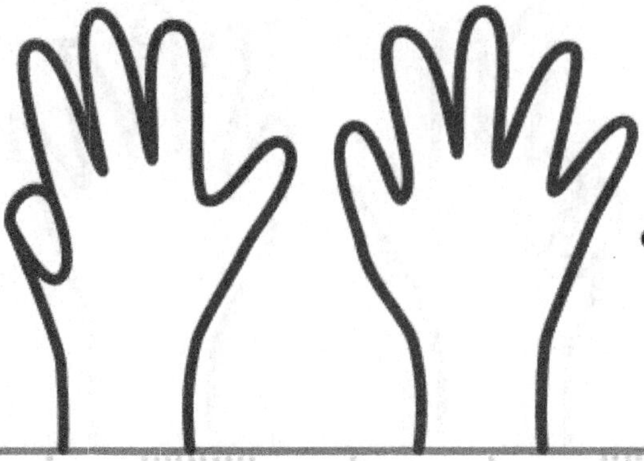

"Nine" is
"Nueve" in Spanish

NINE

9

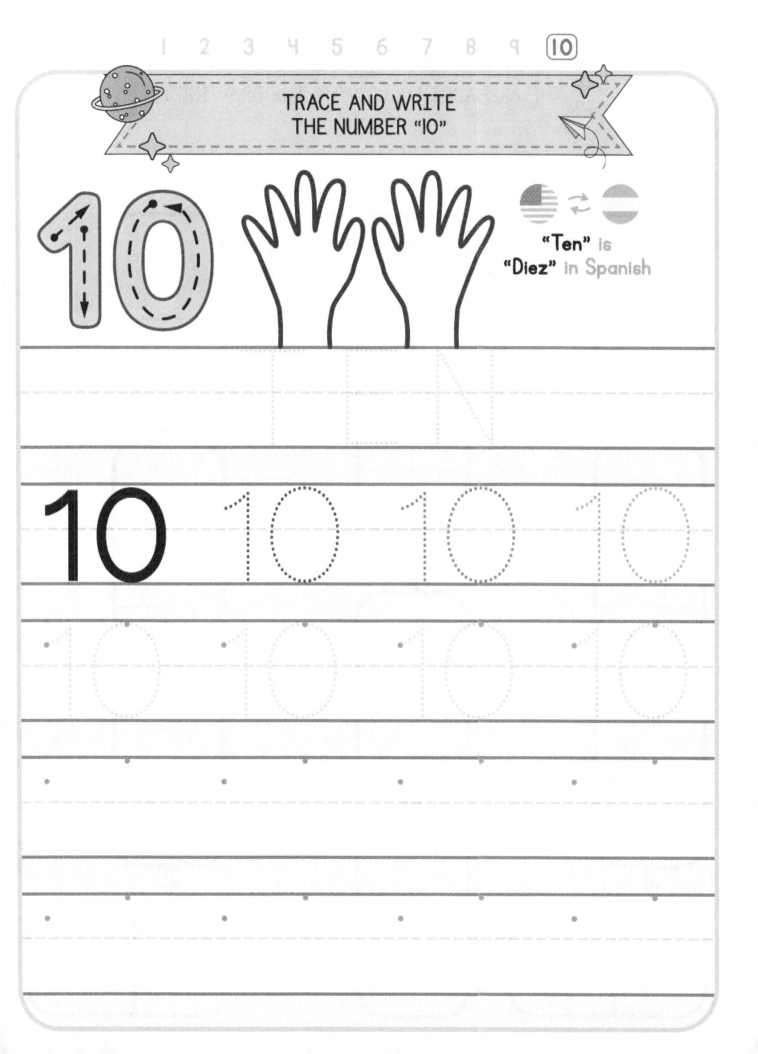

TRACE AND WRITE
THE NUMBER "10"

"Ten" is
"Diez" in Spanish

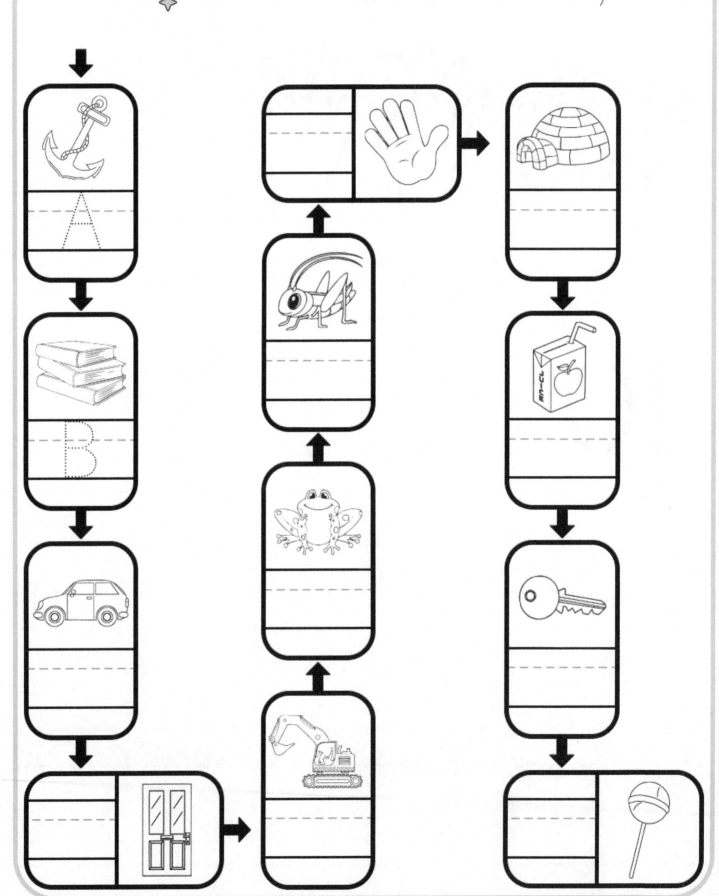

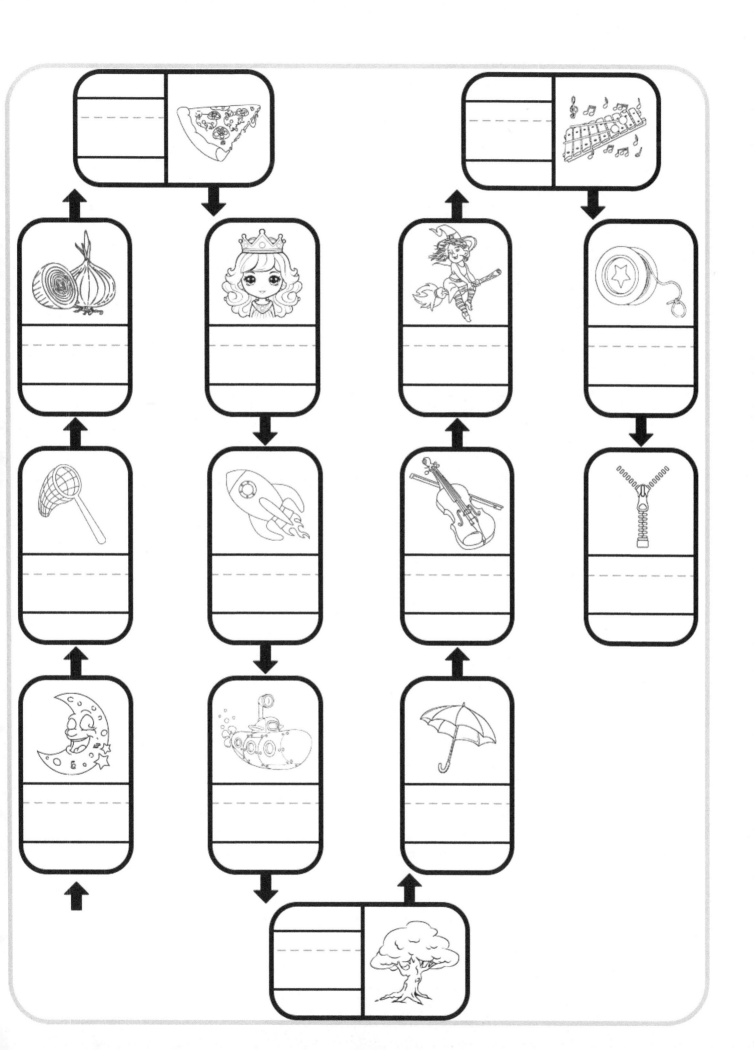

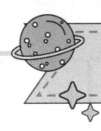

WRITE THEIR NAMES IN UPPERCASE

cat CAT

house

kite

goat

island

nurse

WRITE THEIR NAMES IN LOWERCASE

ZEBRA zebra

SHOES

FOX

TOMATO

WHALE

YARN

MONKEY

MOUSE

JACKET

AIRPLANE

KETCHUP

VAMPIRE

b__cket

__olphin

__rapes

e__epha__t

__ighthou__e

__ushr__om

Made in the USA
Coppell, TX
01 February 2024